John Earl Russell

A Letter to the Right Hon. Chichester Fortescue, M.P. on the

State of Ireland

John Earl Russell

A Letter to the Right Hon. Chichester Fortescue, M.P. on the State of Ireland

ISBN/EAN: 9783744764292

Printed in Europe, USA, Canada, Australia, Japan

Cover: Foto ©Suzi / pixelio.de

More available books at **www.hansebooks.com**

A LETTER

TO THE RIGHT HON.

CHICHESTER FORTESCUE, M.P.

ON

THE STATE OF IRELAND.

BY

JOHN EARL RUSSELL.

'LET RIGHT BE DONE.'

FOURTH EDITION.

LONDON:

LONGMANS, GREEN, AND CO.

1868.

LETTER.

---◆---

My dear Fortescue,

The mind of England has been greatly disturbed of late by Fenian outrages.

The rescue of a Fenian leader at Manchester, and the murder of a constable, who was shot in the performance of his duties, were followed, as we all remember, by trials for the capital offence of murder; trials conducted with all the solemnity, fairness, and publicity which are characteristic of British justice. Five were convicted of the murder; three were executed. Lord Derby, in his place in the House of Lords, declared that he did not see how the allegation, that the constable had been killed in pursuance of a treasonable purpose, could in any way attenuate the crime of murder. This was considered by all who heard it a reasonable observation.

But in Ireland the impression was very different. Every person with Fenian sympathies considered that the men convicted were patriots, innocent of murder because their purpose was treasonable, and because they had no personal malice against Sergeant Brett, their victim. Processions were organised; crape was worn; hearses were paraded through the streets of

B

Cork and Dublin; and every artifice was used to excite sympathy for the martyrs who had been convicted of murder, and had suffered for their crime.

These unseemly processions were forbidden at Liverpool and in Ireland not a day too soon, and thereupon ceased. They were not public meetings for the purpose of passing resolutions, or agreeing to petitions or addresses; they were simply demonstrations against law, justice, and the Queen's authority.

The murder of men, women, and children, belonging to the working classes, which took place at Clerkenwell prison, is another of these Fenian outrages; and, although disavowed by the Fenian councils both here and in America, is clearly entitled to the same pretended defence as the Manchester murder, that it was perpetrated for a treasonable purpose.

I may add that I was informed, two years ago, by a gentleman who had been present at a Fenian council at New York, that the plan there approved was, a plan not to attempt an open rebellion, but to alarm the British Government by constant surprises and outrages, till the time should come when insurrection might be hopeful.

But it is clear that, if the word be given throughout Great Britain and Ireland that desultory outrages and surprises are to be attempted, no one can pretend to direct the precise course of such crimes; and that it is vain to deny the responsibility of atrocious murders when, by the mistake or inexperience of a volunteer miscreant, the Fenian convicts are not rescued, and innocent women and children are destroyed by the traitors whose general purpose of treason and slaughter has been whetted in the secret meetings at New York.

I should think every one would agree that the first thing to be done is to administer the laws in force, and use the weapons in our hands with vigour and with vigilance.

At the first of the late outbreaks, it appears that our long habits of internal peace, and obedience to lawful authority, had dulled the ears, and benumbed the arms of the guardians of order. But of late I remark with pleasure a notable improvement. I read in the 'Times' of the 10th of January last, that when the prisoners Burke, Casey, and Shaw were brought up for examination in Bow Street, previous to their committal for trial, the following measures were adopted :—

Extra precautions had been taken against any attack for the purpose of rescue. The street was cleared, and guarded by double lines of armed constables, stretching across the road above and below the court. The van was escorted by about forty mounted police, armed with cutlasses and revolvers. Armed constables thronged the passages of the court, and a double reserve was kept at the station.

This is a laudable increase of vigilance. It is painful to reflect that, had precautions half as efficient been taken at Manchester in proper time, it is probable that Kelly would not have escaped, Brett would not have been shot, the execution of the three murderers would not have occurred, and the cry of martyrdom would not have been raised in Ireland. Such laxity is much to be lamented.

While, however, every precaution ought to be taken, and persons convicted of crime ought to bear the full penalty of their offences, it behoves us neither to exaggerate the danger, nor to mistake the proper remedies to be applied.

I cannot but see with some alarm the tendency to inflame national animosity against the Irish, and to involve the whole of that nation in the charge not only of disaffection, but of conspiracy and treason. Thus, one correspondent to the *Times* calling himself ' A Briton,' calls attention to 'unspoken words,' and these words are ' Martial Law; ' another correspondent, 'Aliquis,' wants to colonise Ireland with Englishmen, and to make enemies and outlaws of the whole Irish race.

Before we give way to these wild passions of fear and hatred, ought we not to ask ourselves whether anything of the kind has ever taken place in England?

In my time, though not in that of most of my readers, disaffection prevailed in many parts of England.   Wild schemes were afloat: one set of men planned taking the Tower of London with a stocking filled with gunpowder; another set conspired to murder the Cabinet Ministers while they were dining together at Lord Harrowby's; and were actually arming for that horrid purpose, when they were arrested by a detachment of the Guards.   Nothing more atrocious than this Cato Street conspiracy can well be imagined.

The general state of the country in those years is thus shortly described by Sir Henry Bulwer, in his interesting and instructive work, called 'Historical Characters':—

The sovereign and the administration were unpopular—the people generally ignorant and undisciplined—neither the one nor the other understanding the causes of the prevalent disaffection, nor having any idea as to how it should be dealt with.*

The artisans of Manchester thought at that time of marching to London, each with a blanket on his shoulder; Lord Castlereagh introduced bills which he called ' measures of severe coercion.' Both people and Government were wrong: the distress passed away; the disaffection was cured by prosperity and improved administration. No one then thought of saying, that the Cato Street conspiracy was owing to the wickedness of the English people, and required ' martial law' as its remedy.

It seems to me, now that the first panic has passed away, and Parliament is about to meet, that we ought to seek to divest our minds of exaggerated fears and national animosities; to consider patiently all the facts relating to Ireland; to listen to those Irish representatives who, like yourself, would apply healing measures and impartiality where others ask only for martial law and severity; that we ought to weigh with care the complaints that are made, and examine with still more care and circumspection the remedies

* *Historical Characters*, vol. ii. p. 158.

that are proposed, lest, in our attempts to cure the disease, we give the patient a new and more dangerous disorder. I rejoice, therefore, to see the following sensible and patriotic observations, in the charge of the Recorder of Birmingham to the Grand Jury of that town:—

Outrages like those committed at Manchester, or at the Middlesex House of Correction, have raised in the minds of many such a storm of indignation against all persons of Irish extraction, that I dread lest the feeling should degenerate into a war of races or creeds, the results of which could not fail to be highly detrimental to the interest of liberty all over the world ; and I would warn you that it would be most unjust to treat all our fellow-subjects who have come from Ireland as disaffected, or to consider that all who profess the Roman Catholic religion are engaged in treasonable practices, for we have seen the strongest resistance made to adverse forces by native-born Irishmen, and we know that all the heads of the Roman Catholic Church have denounced in the strongest terms the acts of the conspirators who have come from other countries to disturb the peace of these realms.*

These are wise observations, and I wish the Ministers of State who have lately spoken in public had uttered sentiments equally forbearing and equally fair towards the Queen's Irish subjects.

I shall now proceed to make my observations on the state of Ireland, and, for the sake of convenience, I will divide this letter into three parts.

The first part will treat of the material and physical condition of Ireland.

* *Times*, Jan. 9, 1868.

The second of its political and moral state.

The third will treat of the course which, in my opinion, ought to be adopted by Parliament in its coming session.

But before I begin these separate portions, I will endeavour to review shortly the political history of Ireland, from the twelfth to the eighteenth century.

In considering the question of Ireland, too much has been said of historical oppressions, and too little of recent remedies.

The ancient oppressions are truly lamentable; but, as I view the historical retrospect, it may be thus stated.

The Normans overthrew the Saxons and conquered England. A century later, Strongbow and his confederate nobles and knights conquered Ireland. For a long time they derived little aid from Henry the Second; but when the English King, in order to confirm his temporal authority, brought to his assistance the spiritual arm of the Roman Catholic Church, he proclaimed the Pope as head of the Church, and instituted tithes to be paid to the Roman Catholic clergy. It was therefore from the Norman conquerors of Ireland, at the time of the Conquest, and not from the Irish people, that the Roman Catholic Church obtained its property in Ireland. Till the Reformation this property was held by the Catholic Church. But in the reign of Elizabeth all was changed. The Queen, however reluctant, felt herself compelled to acknowledge the soundness of the opinion affirmed by Bacon and by Cecil, that the only friends to her throne, and her title to the Crown, were the Protestants. In relating the events of the year 1570, Froude says :—

> On the morning of the 15th of May, the Bull declaring Elizabeth deposed, and her subjects absolved from their allegiance, was found nailed against the Bishop of London's door, and whatever the Catholic powers might do or not do, the Catholic Church had formally declared war.*

But while any favour to Roman Catholics was at that time full of danger, Elizabeth is justly open to censure for not using any proper means for promoting the Reformation in Ireland, and, in case of failure, for not leaving the Catholic Church undisturbed. 'The churches,' says Hallam, 'were allowed to go to ruin; the benefices fell to strangers, or to conforming ministers of native birth, dissolute and ignorant, as useless to teach as the people were predetermined not to listen.'†

The state of affairs at the commencement of the reign of King William the Third was not very different. The English and Scotch deposed James the Second, and settled the Crowns of England, Ireland, and Scotland upon King William and his heirs, *being Protestants*. The Irish declared for King James, and were defeated at the Battle of the Boyne, at Londonderry, and at Limerick.

That the victory was terribly abused; that laws of proscription were passed; that the two Houses of the

---

* *Froude*, vol. iv. p. 59.
† Hallam, *Const. Hist.*, vol. iii. p. 371, 8vo.

English Parliament vied with one another in cruelty, injustice, and all the refinements of tyranny, it is impossible to deny. Burnet and Edmund Burke have made this melancholy history so clear that no one can doubt the facts.

Yet we cannot wonder that, as Elizabeth would have been murdered if Mary Queen of Scots and Philip the Second had succeeded in their designs, and as William the Third would have lost his life had James the Second prospered in his purpose of assassination, neither Elizabeth nor William felt any inclination to make the Roman Catholic Church the Established Church in Ireland.

What we have to lament, and the Irish to resent, is not so much a victory which was essential to England, as a proscription that was unwise, tyrannical, and destructive to Ireland.

But for what purpose should we now revive those horrible proofs that the cry of *Væ victis*! animated the conquerors of the reigns of Elizabeth and of William?

In Scotland just laws and impartial government have erased from the mind ' the written troubles of the brain.' The perfidy of the Plantagenets, the tyranny of the Tudors, the oppression and duplicity of the Stuarts, and even the Massacre of Glencoe, have all been effaced. Instead of recalling the past woes of Ireland, ought we not to use the example of William and of Somers in their conduct to Scotland as a guide in our conduct towards Ireland?

In pursuing the inquiry which I wish to make, I

propose, in the first place, to mark the material and physical wants of the Irish people; to note the measures taken of late years for the improvement of their condition, and to comment upon the measures suggested to promote their progress to well-being.

PART I.

LET us now, therefore, follow the course of legislation and government which has tended to cause or to
cure the material and physical misery of Ireland.
About 1760 began that contest for the occupation of
land which, in the reign of Henry VIII., had begun
to afflict England.*

In England the great increase of trade, industry,
and the introduction of the Poor Law of the 43rd of
Elizabeth, maintained order and promoted the progress of society.

In Ireland the increase of trade and the growth of
manufactures were nipped in the bud by the jealousy
of England. No Poor Law was introduced; and
from 1760 to 1829 the creation of fagot freeholds
augmented greatly the struggle for small patches of
land, from which alone the means of living were to
be obtained.

Hence the murders, the agrarian outrages, the
crimes against person and property of which Sir
George Lewis has left so frightful a catalogue in his
volume on 'Crime and Disturbance in Ireland.'

The remedies have been due partly to the Divine
Providence and partly to human exertions. Many

---

* See More's *Utopia*, for an account of English evictions.

years ago the Political Economy Club of London came, as I was told, to a resolution that the emigration of two millions of the population of Ireland would be the best cure for her social evils. Famine and emigration have accomplished a task beyond the reach of legislation or government; and Providence has justly afflicted us by the spectacle of the results of the entire dependence on potato cultivation, and by the old fires of disaffection which had been lighted in the hearts of Irishmen, and are now burning with such fierceness on the banks of the Hudson and the Potomac.

The census of 1834 gave the population of Ireland as 7,954,760; that of 1861, as 5,798,957. Thus two millions have been removed by the great famine of 1847–8 and the drain of emigration of the last twenty years.

But, has Parliament been inactive and indifferent? Let us see what measures of legislation have preceded and followed the effects of famine and emigration. A principal subject of inquiry for the ministry of Lord Melbourne was the question whether a Poor Law should be introduced. But as a Poor Law implies a poor rate, this was not to be done without laying a deep foundation by inquiry and statistics. Mr. Nicholl, who for his ability and experience had been appointed one of the Commissioners of Poor Laws in England, was chosen for this inquiry. In 1836 Mr. Nicholl reported 'that there were 2,385,000 persons in Ireland insufficiently provided with the common necessaries of life, and requiring relief for thirty weeks in the year, owing to the want of work; and that the wives and children of many others were obliged to beg systematically, while mendicancy was the sole resource of the aged and impotent.'

While no provision is made for the aged and impotent, the State cannot with justice prohibit begging; while the sturdy beggar is not set to work, the State cannot efficiently prevent the pilfering, imposture, and intimidation which this class of marauders inflicts upon the country.

Such were the evils which were rife in England at the commencement of the sixteenth century; such were the evils which the 43rd of Elizabeth was wisely framed to cure.

Proceeding on the principles adopted by the able statesmen of the reign of Elizabeth, the government of Lord Melbourne, in the year 1837, introduced their bill. The death of the king put a stop to it, but in 1838 it was again introduced. It was opposed by many of the Irish Tories, who looked upon it as a confiscation of landed property, and by Mr. O'Connell, who in speeches of great eloquence and ability denounced this method of remedying Irish grievances. But the measure passed, and having been amended in 1847, is now considered a permanent institution.

An able writer has pointed out that the Poor Law of Ireland does not give the same right to relief which is comprised in the English Act. But I have no space to pursue that discussion.* When I had the honour to explain the proposal for the Irish Poor

* *State of Ireland*, by John Th. Ingram, LL.D., 1864.

Law to King William IV., he remarked, benevolently
and sagaciously, that the bringing together Protestants and Roman Catholics as members of the
Boards of Guardians, would, he hoped, have a tendency to soften religious animosities, and teach the
members of different creeds to act together in harmony for a work of charity.

A measure passed about the same time related to a
grievance which was at once a material and a political
wrong—I speak of the law for the commutation of
tithes.

The measure adopted dealt only with the material
mischief. The collection of tithes in Ireland before
the Union is thus described by Mr. Grattan:—

> The use of the tithe farmer is to get from the parishioners
> what the parson would be ashamed to demand, and to enable
> the parson to absent himself from his duty. The powers of
> the tithe farmer are summary laws and ecclesiastical courts;
> his livelihood is extortion ; his rank in society is generally the
> lowest, and his occupation is to pounce on the poor in the
> name of the Lord! He is a species of wolf left by the shep-
> herd to take care of the flock in his absence.

In another speech Mr. Grattan calls the tithe col-
lectors 'a subordination of vultures.'

Mr. Wakefield, in his elaborate and impartial volumes upon Ireland, describes the consternation of
a village when a half-famished cottier had his cow
seized for tithes:—

> I have heard, with emotions I can scarcely describe, deep
> curses repeated from village to village as the cavalcade pro-
> ceeded; I have beheld at night houses in flames, and for a

moment supposed myself in a country exposed to the usages
of war, and suffering from the incursions of an enemy. On the
following morning the most alarming accounts of Thrashers
and Whiteboys have met my ears—of men who had assembled with weapons of destruction for the purpose of compel-
ling people to swear not to submit to the payment of tithes.
I have been informed of these oppressed people having, in the
ebullition of their rage, murdered both proctors and collec-
tors, wreaking their vengeance with every mark of the most
savage barbarity.*

In 1831 the tithe war, which had been hitherto a
species of guerilla warfare, marking every winter
with a stain of blood, broke out in a more aggravated
form. If I remember right, it began by the seizure,
in the parish of Graigue, of the cow of the priest who
was the religious teacher of the people, in the name
and in pursuance of the claim of the clergyman of
the Established Church, whose teachings the people
refused to hear.

Many fierce encounters dyed the fields of Ireland
with blood.

At Newtown Barry, in the county of Wexford,
the peasantry having assembled to rescue some cattle
impounded by a tithe proctor, the yeomanry fired
upon them, killing twelve persons.

At Carrickshock a fearful slaughter took place.
A number of process-servers, guarded by a strong
body of police, having proceeded to execute the law,
the surrounding hills were crowned with bonfires,
and an immense multitude of the peasantry, armed
with scythes and pitchforks, marched boldly to the

---

* Wakefield's *Account of Ireland*, vol. ii. p. 486.

attack. In a few minutes eighteen of the police, including the commanding officer, were killed.

At Castle Pollard, in the county of Westmeath, the chief constable having been knocked down, the police fired, and nine or ten persons were killed.

At Gartroe, near Rathcormack, in the county of Cork, on an attempt to enforce the payment of tithes from a widow named Ryan, the people resisted, the military fired, eight persons were killed, and thirteen wounded: among the killed was the widow's son.

In this sad conflict, while the track of blood marked the path of the tithe proctor, the Protestant clergy-man was often reduced to beggary, the ties of charity which bound him and his family to his poorer neigh-bours were broken, and he often fled in dismay to the large town where he might find protection, and sleep secure. Sixty thousand pounds were voted by Parliament for the relief of those despoiled clergymen, and the State undertook to levy the arrears which were unpaid. But this campaign, carried on by horse and foot, amid hooting, jeers, and popular in-timidation at every auction and on every farm, was singularly unsuccessful. The amount of the arrears was computed to be 104,285*l.*; the amount recovered was 12,000*l.*, and the cost of collection was 15,000*l.*

It was desirable on every account to put an end to the tithe war. But the question arose, whether it would not be wise to seize the opportunity for de-priving the Church, which was not the Church of the people, of some of those funds which could not be used for spiritual instruction. To this contest I shall advert when I arrive at the political part of this letter. At present I confine myself to the question of material progress.

I will here record, therefore, that in 1838 a bill for the commutation of tithes in Ireland passed both Houses of Parliament. By this Act the landlords were made the creditors of the tithe payers, and the debtors of the tithe owners, receiving 25 per cent. for the risk and trouble of collection.

The tithe war has since ceased; the evils deplored by Mr. Grattan have disappeared; the landlord collects his rents, including the tithe rent-charge, without a conflict, and the clergyman has no longer the odious task of enforcing small payments by police and military aid.

There existed another impost, of small amount but of a peculiarly vexatious nature. This was the church cess—a tax applicable to the vestments, the bread and wine, and the maintenance of the buildings used for Protestant worship. Constant contests arose on the subject of this odious impost. It was happily altogether abolished by the Church Temporalities Act, introduced by the present Lord Derby.

There was another evil intimately connected with the poverty of Irish tenants, and the bad cultivation of Irish farms. This was the deeply encumbered state of Irish landed property. Landlord after landlord, of the kind so well described by Miss Edgeworth in 'Castle Rackrent,' had drunk oceans of claret, entertained with reckless hospitality, mortgaged their estates within a few pounds of the whole rental, and lived as popular pauperised proprietors. The natural consequence was, that these lavish jovial landlords could neither afford to improve their land, nor to forgive a deserving but distressed tenant any part of his arrears. Anxious to remedy this evil, the Government proposed a bill, but the technical rules and maxims of the Court of Chancery stood in the way of an effectual remedy. On going to Ireland to inquire into the working of an Act which Parliament had passed, I was told on the highest authority that the Act would be evaded and inoperative. This was too true a prediction: the first encumbrancer stood in the way, and forbade any efficient application of the new law.

At this time Sir Robert Peel, in a speech of great ability, propounded a scheme of his own upon the subject; but his views were not, in the opinion of the persons most capable of judging, likely to prove practically beneficial.

In this strait Sir John Romilly, one of the law officers of the Crown, undertook to revise the whole subject, and framed a measure which was brought forward in the name of the Government, was highly praised by Sir Robert Peel, and, being passed, laid the foundation of a beneficent legislation in a matter of the deepest importance. Property of the value of thirty millions has changed masters in consequence of this and supplementary Acts. I may here briefly state the effect of these and some concomitant changes acting at the same time with a large voluntary emigration.

1. The landlord very seldom finds, on the expiration of a lease, that his estate is so crowded with pauper tenants as to induce him to have recourse to one of those wholesale evictions of which the circumstances are so painful and so dreadful.

2. The middleman having in a great measure disappeared, the landlord receives a better rent, while the tenant is less pinched by the landlord's demands. For instance, the late Lord Duncannon found a part of his estate let to a middleman, who paid him 15s. an acre, while he received from the tenant 25s. The lease expired; Lord Duncannon let the land for 20s. an acre, the tenant paying 5s. less, and the landlord receiving 5s. more.

3. Improving tenants are far more common than they were, and more generally encouraged by the landlord. Even those who are esteemed absentee landlords frequently pass a considerable portion of the recess of Parliament in Ireland, and are able to inspect the farms, and encourage and assist their improving tenants. In 1801, the Duke of Devonshire, Lord Fitzwilliam, and Lord Bessborough seldom visited Ireland. The passage by sea was long; the posting by road tedious; their neighbours few, and their houses uncomfortable. At the present time, the owners of these titles frequently visit Ireland, do much good, and are, together with their families, very popular.

4. The labourer receives in many counties 9s. a week; in 1831 he scarcely found employment at 5s. a week.

5. The pauper has a secure refuge in a workhouse where he need not fear to starve. The Poor Law Commissioners, totally unconnected with politics, perform their duties firmly and impartially.

6. The number of evictions has very materially diminished.

As illustrations of the statements I have made, I will now add some information, partly derived from official returns furnished to me by the favour of the Irish Government departments, and partly from works of known reputation and authority. I am sorry that I cannot carry back the criminal returns to 1831; but none were made to Dublin Castle till 1844, the previous reports having been made to the four provincial inspectors.

RETURN OF AGRARIAN OUTRAGES SPECIALLY REPORTED THROUGHOUT IRELAND DURING THE YEARS 1844, 1851, 1861, 1865, 1866:—

	1844	1845	1861	1865	1866
Homicide	18	12	4	4	—
Firing at the person . . .	26	13	4	2	3
Assault endangering life . .	12	2	5	4	4
Assault on bailiffs and process-servers	—	3	—	—	—
Incendiary fire	121	185	25	48	29
Taking and holding forcible possession	7	2	—	—	—
Killing or maiming cattle . .	54	56	17	11	6
Demand or robbery of arms .	9	7	—	1	—
Appearing armed . . .	17	5	1	1	—
Riot	5	2	1	—	1
Threatening letters . . .	417	395	105	73	32
Attacking houses . . .	84	20	2	3	1
Resistance to legal process . .	18	25	1	—	—
Injury to property . . .	69	54	25	15	6
Firing into dwellings . . .	31	18	8	—	1
	888	799	198	162	83

POOR RELIEF, IRELAND, 1841, 1844–47, 1848–51, 1861–65, 1867 :—

Year	Population	Total number relieved in-door	Total number relieved out-door	Total number relieved in-door and out-door during the year
1841	8,199,853	31,108	—	—
1844	8,276,627	104,409	—	—
Sept. 29, 1847	8,025,274	420,499	14,000	434,499
Out-door relief, commenced Sept. 1847				
1848	7,639,800	610,463	1,433,042	2,043,505
1851	6,514,473	707,443	47,914	755,357
1861	5,788,415	203,422	14,008	217,430
1865	5,641,086	252,170	36,826	288,996
1867	5,556,962	257,890	55,000	312,890

Let me now give some figures on the rate of wages, taken from Lord Dufferin's work on 'Irish Emigration' :—

	1867.
Antrim	8*s.*
Carlow	7*s.*
Cork	7*s.* to 8*s.*
Galway	7*s.*
Kildare	9*s.*
Kerry	7*s.*
,, (in summer) . . .	9*s.*
Meath	7*s.* to 8*s.*
Tipperary	7*s.* to 8*s.*

The following rest on official authority :—

RETURNS OF RATE OF WAGES IN SOME OF THE PRINCIPAL AGRICULTURAL DISTRICTS :—

	1831	1841	1851	1861	1866
Near Athy, co. Kildare . . .	little money wages	4*s.* to 5*s.*	7*s.*	8*s.*	8*s.*
Near Clogheen, south part of co. Tipperary . . .	5*s.*	6*s.*	7*s.*	8*s.*	8*s.*

Returns of Rate of Wages in some of the principal Agricultural Districts (*continued*):—

	1831	1841	1851	1861	1886
Lurgan, co. Armagh	6s.	—	—	—	9s.
Near New Ross, co. Wexford and Kilkenny	5s. to 6s.	5s. to 6s.	6s.	6s. to 7s.	6s. to 7s.
Near Castlerea, cos. Roscommon and Mayo, winter	4s.	4s.	6s.	7s. 6d.	8s.
Same, summer	6s.	6s.	9s.	10s.	12s.
Near Killarney, co. Kerry	4s.	5s.	5s.	6s.	7s.

The following table is taken from Dr. Hancock's interesting work on the ' Supposed Decline of Irish Prosperity,' published in 1863*:—

The Number of Evictions, as ascertained by the Police, in each Year, from 1849 to 1862, compared with the Number of Persons permanently leaving Ireland:—

Years	Number of evictions		Number of persons permanently leaving Ireland
	Families	Persons	
1849	13,384	72,065	254,425 ⎫
1850	14,546	74,171	249,050 ⎬ †
1851	8,815	43,449	289,721 ⎭
1852	6,550	32,160	190,322 ⎫
1853	3,820	17,868	173,148	
1854	1,835	8,980	140,555	
1855	1,365	6,732	91,914	
1856	878	3,948	90,781	
1857	919	4,223	95,081 ⎬ ‡
1858	720	3,432	64,337	
1859	491	2,348	80,599	
1860	511	2,711	87,626	
1861	829	3,964	66,396	
1862	983	4,972	72,730 ⎭

* *Report on the Supposed Progressive Decline of Irish Prosperity.* By W. Neilson Hancock, L.L.D.

† These numbers are obtained by adding an estimated average number of persons migrating to England and Scotland to the numbers emigrating abroad.

‡ These figures are taken from the Emigration Returns published by the Registrar-General for Ireland.

With respect to the number of holdings in Ireland not exceeding one acre, and between one and five acres, in the year 1866, I have the following return:—

	Not exceeding one acre	Between one and five acres	Total not above five acres
1866	48,236	79,742	127,978

The Irish labourer was long deprived of that resource which the English farmer's son of a large family, or labourer without employment, found in Warwickshire, Yorkshire, or Lancashire. English legislation prohibited competition with English manufactures; but the facilities of locomotion, and a change in our laws, have greatly improved the Irishman's condition. An Irishman goes to London in few hours, and at small expense. Leeds, Manchester, Birmingham, teem with Irish. Five-and-thirty years ago, in the case of distress, the Irish labourers were sent back to Ireland under the Poor Law Removal Acts ; but at present, if they have been able to support themselves for three years, they are entitled to relief in the place of their residence. The consequence is, that about one-fourth of the destitute relieved by the poor-rates in Birmingham are Irish. The Irish have, in fact, the resource in our manufacturing towns which the English have long enjoyed, and our unworthy jealousy has been righteously defeated.

In considering the vexed question of the relation of landlord and tenant, we are met (as in all Irish questions) by theorists, who wish to treat Ireland as a sheet of white paper, and write on it, with the utmost confidence that they will be believed and followed by all the idle inhabitants of our watering-places—

> Et otiosa credidit Neapolis
> Et omne vicinum oppidum.

'Let us give fixity of tenure,' say many, meaning thereby, 'Let us transfer the property of the land from the owner to the tenant.' Yet this cannot be done with any regard to the rights of property, or the interests of the whole country.

The question of the tenure of land is one much more of prevailing customs and of habits, made up partly of law and partly of tradition, than a matter of positive institution, like representative assemblies and judicial tribunals.

If we go to Prussia, which is held up for our imitation, we find that serfdom existed in Prussia to a late period, that the tenant had a customary right to occupation, and had certain feudal services to perform in return. Baron Stein, in 1807, made an equitable arrangement between the landlord and the occupier, giving compensation to the landlord, and a secure property to the occupier.

But these military feudal tenures were abolished in England 200 years ago,* and property has since been held, generally speaking, by a freehold or copyhold tenure. The same freehold tenure prevails in Ireland. Thus, this comparison entirely fails.

In Spain, where large wild tracts are barren, Mr.

---

* 12 Car. II. c. 24. 'A statute,' says Blackstone, ' which was a greater acquisition to the civil property of this kingdom than even Magna Charta itself.'—*Blackstone*, b. ii. c. 5.

Frere, a very poetical diplomatist said, 'For my part, I like a country where God Almighty keeps a good deal of land in His own hands.' But, except in Valencia, where the Moors created fertility by irrigation, and Christians have carried much further the Moorish system, there is little to be learnt from Spain.

If we look to Italy, we may find there the skilful cultivation of the territory of Lucca described in Lalande's 'Travels'; the system of Tuscany, where the landlord pays half the expense of preparing the crop, and is paid by half the produce, a system condemned by Baron Ricasoli; the large dairy farms of Lombardy, and the wretched agriculture of the Pope's narrow territory; with various other systems flowing from various forms of law and government.

If we look to France, we find 7,000,000 of proprietors and 120,000,000 of properties. Undoubtedly, if the state of French agriculture be compared with the miserable condition of agricultural industry before the Revolution, great progress has been made; but if the agriculture of France be compared with that of England or Scotland, France has much to learn and much to lament.

In Belgium there is a system of very high rents and very short leases—a system which, springing from the days of the republics of Flanders and Brabant, has produced, as its results, prodigious industry and enormous produce. But the incessant labour of the Belgian occupier is the growth of centuries, and could not be introduced into Ireland by an Act of the 30th of Victoria.

Let us now turn to England, Scotland, and

Ireland—the three large divisions of the United Kingdom.

In England, generally speaking, the tenants of the great landholders have no leases, because they prefer to be without leases. Lord Althorp told me, that when he came into possession of his property as Earl Spencer, he offered leases to all his tenants, and they all refused. The reason is clear. If he had granted, in 1836, leases for twenty-one years, those leases would have expired in 1857, and his successor might then have resolved on a fresh valuation, and have offered a renewal of the leases at a higher rent. I believe this feeling is common.

But while the English tenant-farmers do not wish to have leases, they are very ready to vote with their landlords at an election for the county. No actual compulsion is requisite for this purpose; but I will not undertake to say to what degree the tenants may be influenced by personal attachment, by regard for an old family with which they have been long connected, by agreement with their landlord in political opinions, or by a wish to secure the favour of his agent. All I venture to assert is, that there is very little actual compulsion in the case; and I doubt whether the introduction of the ballot would make much practical difference.

In Scotland the case is different. I may be suspected of political heresy if I assert, what however I believe to be the fact, that the restriction of the franchise in Scotch counties to a limited number of landowners (about 3000 in all Scotland), from 1688 to 1831, tended to the rapid improvement of Scotch

agriculture. The tenant having no vote, the landlord's sole object was to obtain a good rent, and have
his land improved. Hence leases for nineteen, twenty-
one, or more years; hence the security of the tenant
during the period of his lease; hence his intelligence,
his skill, and his quickness in turning every circum-
stance to account; so that, if, at the end of his lease, a
new tenant were preferred to him, he might be amply
recompensed for his outlay.

The case of Ireland has been lamentably different.
The small farmer, for centuries past, having no resource in Cork or Kilkenny similar to that of the
English agricultural population in Manchester, Birmingham, Leeds, and the Lancashire and Yorkshire
towns, sought his livelihood from the land alone. If
he obtained a lease, he divided his farm among his
sons and sons-in-law, his brothers and brothers-in-
law. This practice no doubt tended neither to the
improvement of the land, nor to the comfortable and
respectable position of the tenants. But the English
legislators, whose ancestors had shut him out from the
woollen manufacture, from trade to the East and
West Indies, and even from the exportation of cattle
to England, and thus cut off all inducement to improve his condition by learning to weave cloth, or
engage in commerce, have no right to blame him if
jealousy and injustice have produced idleness and
improvidence.

There was another source of evil for the tenantry
of Ireland—the political franchises, instead of being
too restricted as in Scotland, were too far extended.

Hence, after the admission of Roman Catholics to

the franchise in 1792, it became the practice to create 40s. freeholders, not by tens and twenties, but by hundreds and by thousands, and to march these two-legged cattle up to the poll to support the land-owner's favourite candidate, and to enable him to carry those jobs at the Castle which he might have in hand at the time.   Sir R. Peel, in 1829, in moving the Roman Catholic Relief Bill, after stating the very moderate number of voters in English counties, said, ' I believe there are many counties in Ireland in which fourteen or fifteen thousand voters are registered, and some counties in which there are upwards of twenty thousand.'*

But in the same speech Sir R. Peel recorded the result of this abuse :—

It is in vain to deny or to conceal the truth in respect to that franchise.   It was until a late period the instrument through which the landed aristocracy, the resident and the absentee proprietor, maintained their local influence—through which property had its weight, its legitimate weight, in the national representation.   The landlord has been disarmed by the priest; and the fear of spiritual denunciations, acting in unison with the passions and feelings of the multitude, has already severed in some cases, and will sever in others, unless we interfere to prevent it, every tie between the Protestant proprietor and the lower class of his Roman Catholic tenantry. That weapon which he has forged with so much care, and has heretofore wielded with so much success, has broken short in his hand.†

The Government of 1829 proposed to raise the freehold franchise from 40s. to 10l. Lord Duncannon,

---

* *Hansard*, vol. xx.   † *Hansard*, vol. xx. March 5, 1829.

on the second reading, observed that but for the constitutional exercise of their privileges by the 40*s.* freeholders of Louth, Waterford, and Clare this bill would never have been heard of. But the abuse was flagrant, and some remedy was required. The remedy proposed indeed restricted the elective franchise within very narrow limits. But in 1850 a measure was carried through Parliament granting the franchise to occupiers rated at twelve pounds a year.

Still the fight—the fight for life and death—continued. Mr. Shiel described it dramatically somewhat in this fashion:—

Timothy Nolan is accosted by his landlord, Mr. Martin, a deposit of the Lord Protector. 'Who do you vote for, Tim?' 'For O'Connell, plase your honour.' 'Who told you to vote for O'Connell?' 'Father O'Shaugnessy, plase your honour.' 'Father O'Shaugnessy! What has he to do with your vote? Remember, Tim, you have no lase!'

And if he does not remember it, and votes as the priest bids him, he is ejected from his rude dwelling, and loses all the produce of the ten or fifteen acres, which in a course of years he has cultivated with patient industry, and whereby alone he procures sustenance for his wife and children.

This is a subject which requires the application of sound general principles, but likewise, let me add, of sound common sense. For instance, let us suppose for a minute that all the difficulties of converting tenants into landlords were overcome, and then consider what would be the practical consequences of establishing in England and Ireland some legal and equitable mode of creating a great number of small landholders, say of twenty acres each, and of the yearly value of one pound per acre.   The English freeholder, acting on the principle of free trade in land, finding that his twenty acres would sell at forty years' purchase, and that at 5 per cent. he would obtain forty pounds a year, and at 4 per cent. thirty-two pounds a year, would sell his land.   He would easily find a secure investment at 4 per cent., and a tolerably secure one at 5 per cent.   His family would rejoice; and the difference of income would be to him of much more importance than the freehold franchise; while the buyer, being probably a large proprietor, would be willing to get 2 or $2\frac{1}{2}$ per cent. for his purchase-money, and would consider the convenience of having twenty acres of preserve for his game bordering on, or perhaps enclosed in, his large estate of more importance than the difference of income.   In Ireland, on the other hand, the small landowner would keep his freehold, and would take advantage of his property to introduce numerous sons, sons-in-law, and brothers-in-law on the twenty acres, not one of whom would improve the land, not one of whom would maintain that degree of comfort and ease which bespeaks a happy, instructed, and contented people.   Thus, in England the progress of absorption by the rich would go on; while Ireland would make a large retrograde step, and old evils and old miseries, a wretched tenantry, low wages, ragged clothing, and precarious subsistence would re-appear in all their deformity.

The State, as it appears to me, without interfering

unnecessarily with the acquisition or distribution of wealth, may fairly look to the observance of these general rules. First, that property should have its rights and perform its duties. Second, that the tenants of landowners should live in comfort and security. Third, that a produce should be obtained from the land representing fair if not very skilful cultivation.

These conditions are the result of good government, and its proof.

Looking to the state of Ireland, it is impossible to say that these conditions are performed. Property does not fully perform its duties while there are proprietors who wantonly evict good careful tenants on the ground that they have voted conscientiously at a county election. Nor can the tenant be said to live in security and comfort while he is liable to so capricious an exercise of power on the part of his landlord.

Nor is the land fairly cultivated when the tenant has neither the security of a lease, nor a capital which he can lay out on his land with any certainty of reckoning on the return upon which the English and Scotch tenant may justly calculate.

On this complicated and difficult subject I know no remedy better than that afforded by your Bill. If the tenant has not a lease, he is fully entitled to compensation for his improvements in case of arbitrary eviction. The objection put forward on the part of the Conservative party to a law compensating a tenant for improvements to the making of which the landlord had not previously agreed, has now been withdrawn. It is, therefore, very desirable to settle the question while the present Government remain in office.

The Commission of 1834 expressed a wish in favour of the creation of small properties in land. But since that time the Encumbered Estates Act, and other Acts subsidiary to it, have caused the sale of many millions worth of land. Latterly the high prices given by small capitalists have induced the Commissioners to sell estates in smaller portions. I cannot say that, according to the accounts I have heard, the new small proprietors are remarkable for being liberal landlords.

But, at all events, the property in land is more divided, the proprietors are more numerous, and I have no doubt that improved cultivation will be the result. Very low rents, whether in England, Scotland, or Ireland, generally co-exist with very slovenly cultivation.

There is some difficulty in finding proper judges or arbitrators to decide on questions of compensation in cases of ejectment. The judge of assize can hardly be called upon to give an opinion to a jury in long and intricate cases of this kind; a local court would be suspected of partiality. But gentlemen belonging to the Bar in Dublin might hold circuit courts for this especial purpose, and have power to call in assessors to assist them, both from the landlord and tenant class. They should, I think, have power to award compensation without referring the question to a jury.

There has been much controversy respecting the tenant-right of Ulster. It cannot be a *bonum per se* that a tenant should enter on a farm shorn of half his capital, and having paid nearly the value of the freehold for liberty to cultivate it. But it is an evil to prevent a greater evil: it is inoculation and not vaccination. It is the interest of the landlord, however, not to attempt a violent abolition of this custom; he should rather try to satisfy the out-going tenant himself, and then admit a new tenant with his capital free from payment to his predecessor.

Loans to landlords are in certain cases sanctioned by Parliament. It would be a far better plan to extend this system than to allow the incoming tenant to incur debts before he begins to cultivate his new holding.

I hold the equitable tacit compact between landlord and tenant to go far beyond the law of emblements. Not only when the tenant has sown the land is he entitled to the crop; but when he has so improved the land as to fit it to bear larger and better crops in future years, he is entitled, in my opinion, to the benefit either of a lease long enough to reimburse himself with interest for his outlay, or to obtain from the landlord who has ejected him, that compensation which he has not been allowed to extract from the soil. Such I understand to be the principle of your Bill, and whether it passes under the name of Lord Mayo or your own does not make a material difference.

From this review of the past and present, we may, I think, draw the following conclusions:—

1. That the commutation of tithes, the introduction of poor-laws, the sale of encumbered estates, the

general recognition of the maxim that property has its duties as well as its rights, the more general residence of the proprietors of land in Ireland, the large emigration of the unemployed, and the rise of wages from 4*s*. or 5*s*. to 8*s*. or 9*s*. per week, have greatly tended to improve the condition of Ireland.

2. That, in these circumstances, it is wise to give a security to tenants, by such Bills as yours or Lord Mayo's, that the duties of property will not be violated by the landlord with impunity; that a tenant who improves, if ejected while he pays his rent, is entitled to compensation for his outlay. But that no scheme, violating the rights of property, which we are told were respected by Robespierre and the French Convention,* and which are held sacred by the English nation beyond any other nation, ought to be adopted. That even a plan which, without violating the rights of property, proceeds on the supposition that Irish tenants are what they are not, and that they will do what they will not do, ought to be rejected.

3. That, considering the progress made from 1829 to 1868, we may rely with confidence on the progress to be made from 1868 in another forty years, if justice, peace, and order are maintained, and the moral grievances of Ireland are redressed.

---

* See Quinet, *La Révolution*, vol. ii.

PART II.

I now proceed, therefore, to the political and moral condition of Ireland for a century past, and shall then endeavour to deduce from the narrative of the past, and the aspect of the present, some lessons for the future.

Going back for more than a century, we find that, about the year 1760, the Duke of Bedford, then Lord Lieutenant of Ireland, proposed to his Council a bill, laid before him by Lord Clanbrassil,* for the Regis-tration of Roman Catholic Priests; a measure which, in respect to the Roman Catholics, would have been nearly equivalent in effect to the Act of Toleration in England. But the theory of the law then was, that no Roman Catholics existed in Ireland, and the principle avowed was that they should not be tolerated. The Primate and the Lord Chancellor, the Chief Justice and the Chief Baron, alike opposed the measure; Chief Baron Willes especially denounced the bill, ' because it would prove a toleration of that religion which it had been the general policy of England and of Ireland to persecute and to depress.'

The Duke of Bedford maintained,

That if it would be at all consistent with the peace of society, Christianity and good policy alike required that they

* Ancestor by the female line of the present Earl of Roden.

(the Roman Catholics) should be allowed the exercise of their religious duties. It was his settled maxim that persecution for religious principles only added strength to the sect it was intended to destroy.

But although the Lord-Lieutenant, in a speech of three quarters of an hour, urged his views very strongly, the Privy Council, after a long debate, threw out Lord Clanbrassil's bill by a majority of fourteen to twelve.*

The law which existed in England at this time is thus described by Mr. Burke:—

'A statute was fabricated in 1699, by which the saying mass . . . . . was forged into a crime punishable with perpetual imprisonment. The teaching school, an useful and virtuous occupation, even the teaching in a private family, was in every Catholic subjected to the same unproportioned punishment.' †
This persecuting law was repealed on the motion of Sir George Savile in 1778. It was, I think, upon Lord North's giving his hearty assent to the principles of toleration on which this bill was founded, that Fox quoted with prodigious effect the lines,—

> As one who long in populous city pent,
> Where houses thick and sewers annoy the air,
> Forth issuing on a summer morn to breathe
> Among the pleasant villages and farms
> Adjoined, from each thing met conceives delight, &c.

In 1793 Roman Catholics in Ireland were admitted to the exercise of the elective franchise. This was a

---

* *Correspondence of Duke of Bedford*, vol. ii. Introduction.
† Speech at Bristol, previous to the election.

concession which had been refused the year before with every mark of contempt, and was now yielded solely to fear.

Upon the Union with Ireland, Mr. Pitt, on Jan. 31, 1801, deliberately explained his views in a letter to the King. After saying that he should look to the King's ease and satisfaction, ' in preference to all considerations but those arising from what, in his honest opinion, is due to the real interest of your Majesty and your dominions,' he proceeds thus to state his opinion: 'Under the impression of that opinion, he has concurred in what appeared to be the prevailing sentiments of the majority of the Cabinet, that the admission of the Catholics and Dissenters to offices, and of the Catholics to Parliament (from which latter the Dissenters are not now excluded), would, under certain conditions to be specified, be highly advisable, with a view to the tranquillity and improvement of Ireland, and to the general interest of the United Kingdom.'

The members who formed the majority of the Cabinet here alluded to comprised the most eminent members of the Administration—Lord Grenville and Lord Spencer, Mr. Dundas and Mr. Windham. Mr. Pitt's conditions, some of which were open to objection, comprised a pecuniary provision, under regulation, for the Roman Catholic clergy. The whole plan, modified by counsel and discussion in Parliament, might have laid the foundations for the tranquillity of Ireland, and the increased strength of the empire at the present day.

But the King's mind had unfortunately been poisoned by his Chancellor, Lord Loughborough, and influenced by the authority of the Archbishop of Canterbury; and their opinions had been brought to weigh upon the King's decision by artful intrigues before the large and wise view of Mr. Pitt had been allowed to reach him.

Thus prejudiced, he rejected at once the advice of the minister who for seventeen years had possessed his confidence and the support of a large majority in Parliament.

After a compliment to the integrity and talents of Mr. Pitt, the King proceeds:—

But a sense of religious as well as political duty has made me, from the moment I mounted the throne, consider the oath that the wisdom of our forefathers has enjoined the Kings of this realm to take at their Coronation, and enforced by the obligation of instantly following it, in the course of the ceremony, with taking the Sacrament, as so binding a religious obligation in me to maintain the fundamental maxims on which our Constitution is placed—namely, the Church of England being the established one, and that those who hold employment in the State must be members of it, and, consequently, obliged not only to take oaths against Popery, but to receive the Holy Communion agreeably to the rites of the Church of England.

After confessing his belief in this strange error as to the sense and meaning of the Coronation Oath, the King shows, in another passage, that he had never understood or concurred in the views of his minister in promoting the Union with Ireland:—

When the Irish Propositions were transmitted to me by a

joint message from both Houses of the British Parliament, I told the Lords and Gentlemen sent on that occasion that I would with pleasure and without delay forward them to Ireland, but that, as individuals, I could not help acquainting them that my inclination to a union with Ireland was principally founded on a trust that the uniting the Established Churches of the two kingdoms would for ever shut the door to any further measures with respect to the Roman Catholics.*

The sequel of this strange portion of history is well known. Mr. Addington, who became Prime Minister, fully shared the prejudices of the King. Neither Mr. Pitt, when he returned to power, nor Mr. Fox, and Lord Grenville, who on Mr. Pitt's death took the direction of public affairs, chose to disturb the settled, or rather the unsettled, mind of George the Third. Upon Lord Grenville's retirement from office, the bigotry of Mr. Perceval inflamed the intolerance of the country; and while George the Third was in possession of his faculties, there was no hope of such a measure as Mr. Fox, Mr. Pitt, and all the great statesmen of the time would have approved. During the ministry of Lord Liverpool, the Catholic disabilities were made an open question, and the Commons beheld for years the unedifying spectacle of the Home and Foreign Secretaries of State taking the lead on opposite sides upon a question which vitally concerned the peace and happiness of Ireland, and the stability of the Empire.

At length, in 1828, agitation in Ireland forced on a solution. O'Connell, the most powerful demagogue

* *Stanhope's Pitt*, vol. iii. Appendix xxiii., xxviii.

of any age, kept the people of Ireland on the verge of insurrection, at once denouncing with furious invective the British Government, and forbidding to the people the use of physical force. He was completely successful, and the measure of Roman Catholic Relief was as much Mr. O'Connell's work, as the Repeal of the Corn Laws was Mr. Cobden's, and the Reform Bill of 1867 was Mr. Bright's.

Some evils were sure to arise from the long delay of justice in regard to the Roman Catholic Relief Act, and from the manner in which it was carried. Mr. O'Connell at once began a new agitation for the Repeal of the Union. That excellent prelate, Archbishop Murray, on the first mention of this subject, observed sensibly to Mr. O'Connell that in Catholic Emancipation he was assisted by half England, whereas, on the question of Repeal, he would have the whole of England strongly opposed to him. Mr. O'Connell's reply was, ' You will see that I shall carry Repeal more easily than Emancipation.' But the Archbishop's foresight was fully justified. Lord Althorp, soon after taking office, declared with emphasis that he would resist to the utmost the dismemberment of the Empire; the whole Whig party followed him in a strenuous and successful opposition to the proposal of Repeal. Yet many years were wasted in this sterile agitation, and the beneficial effects which might have been expected in 1801, did not speedily follow the enactment of 1829. Still, when the benefits which have flowed from that measure are considered, they will be found to have been

permanent, largely useful, and extensively concilia-
tory. Catholic peers have taken their seats in the
House of Lords; Catholic orators of the rank of
O'Connell and Shiel have added lustre to the debates
of the House of Commons; Catholic judges have ex-
pounded from the Bench the laws which are the birth-
right of the subject, and awarded the punishment
due to the traitor and the malefactor.

When a Roman Catholic shall take his seat, as Lord
Chancellor of Ireland these benefits of equal justice
will be still more widely possessed by the Irish people.
Even the permission to Roman Catholic judges and
mayors to appear in their places of worship with
their official insignia, long withheld by party and
sectarian prejudice, is not without its value. It is
a part of equality, and equality is signified by a
scarf, no less than by the seals of office, or a seat in
Parliament.

When Lord Grey came into office, and the Whigs,
after sixty years of exclusion, began a new scheme
of Irish policy, there were two prominent evils in the
government of Ireland. The first was the corrupt and
intolerant system of administration called Protestant
Ascendancy; the second, the Irish Church Establishment. The first of these evils—called by Burke, *Non
regnum sed magnum latrocinium*; and by Fox, *a miserable monopolising minority* — was quite as great a
grievance to the people of Ireland as the second.
It drove into rebellion such men as Lord Edward
Fitzgerald, the Emmets, and Wolfe Tone. By a series
of what were called by Irish statesmen 'ripening

measures,' the disaffected classes were irritated, goaded, spurred into insurrection; and when they had rebelled, were tortured, massacred, and shot, till the spirit of disloyalty, if not extirpated, was terrified and subdued.

Hence a state of government, which was described by Lord Redesdale as one law for the rich and another for the poor, and both equally ill administered.

It is worth while indeed to go back a little, in order to borrow the descriptions given by Burke, the Protestant statesman, and Dr. Doyle, the Roman Catholic bishop, of the system of government called Protestant Ascendancy.

Burke writes to his friend Windham, at a time when Lord Fitzwilliam, placing his confidence in Mr. Grattan, was disposed to govern Ireland by his counsels and with his support. Burke protested against the notion that such men as Grattan and Ponsonby were to be distrusted and kept at a distance :—

For it is not to know Ireland to say, that what is called opposition is what will give trouble to a Viceroy. His embarrassments are upon the part of those who ought to be the supports of English government, but who have formed themselves into a cabal to destroy the King's authority, and to divide the country as a spoil amongst one another. ' *Non regnum sed magnum latrocinium,*' the motto which ought to be put under the harp. This is not talk. I can put my hand on the instances, and not a doubt would remain on your mind of the fact.

Again he says:—

The little cliques there are to me as nothing ; they have never done me a favour nor an injury : but that kingdom is of great importance indeed.

Being determined to support Pitt at all hazards, he yet felt deeply the injury his misgovernment was then doing.   He exclaims in agony:—

Oh! my dear friend, I write with a sick heart and a wearied hand. If you can, pluck Ireland out of the unwise and corrupt hands that are destroying us !

He saw very clearly that those who governed on the principles of corruption and intolerance were the best friends of French Jacobinism.

I should have made a great scruple of conscience to do any-thing whatever for the support, directly or indirectly, of a set of men in Ireland, who, that conscience well-informed tells me, by their innumerable corruptions, frauds, oppressions, and follies, are opening a back door for Jacobinism to rush in and to take us in the rear. As surely as you and I exist, so surely this will be the consequence of their persisting in their system.*

Such, according to Mr. Burke, a supporter of Mr. Pitt, was the system of governing Ireland adopted by that Minister.

Let us now see Bishop Doyle's description of this same mode of administration.

There can be no doubt, he says, that till within these very few years every administration of public money or business in Ireland was most corrupt.   There was no faith kept with God or man by those to whom the public interests, or any portion of them, happened to be committed. From the highest tribunals, to the lowest collector of excise, bribery,

* *Diary of the Right Hon. W. Windham,* pp. 326-30.

extortion, perjury prevailed. In all the public offices peculation and plunder were reduced to system—openly avowed and acted upon. The commissioners at the different boards were as regularly fee'd by those who had business to transact with them as they were paid by Government. But the Government itself was the great debauchee. There was no job too gross, no proceeding so licentious, no abuse of power or patronage so glaring, to which its active agency or tacit sanction was not extended. The Church was in perfect keeping with the State; the public offices were dens of thieves; the courts of justice, with their purlieus, were sinks of corruption; and the grand juries throughout the country invited by their practice and example the suitors or claimants at every court of assize in Ireland to disregard both truth and justice, to commit perjury, and to plunder or oppress their neighbour. There is no exaggeration—no high colouring in the foregoing statement. The truth of every portion of it is either already recorded in evidence reported to Parliament, or could be proved by ten thousand living witnesses. This then being till lately the state of Ireland, and of the administration of all her public affairs, it is no wonder that men doubt whether money could be levied equitably, and expended honestly and impartially, even for the benefit of the poor. Let it, however, be considered, and in the first place, that, until within a few years past, an exceedingly small fraction of the people of this country held exclusive possession of the administration of public business in all its diversity and ramifications. That fraction of the people lived by their offices, pensions, sinecures, or employments—they alone constituted society in Ireland—they were all sharers alike in oppression, and each took his portion of the spoil produced by it. They were not ashamed of each other, for no man blushes at his own theft in a company of thieves. There was no Government to exercise control. The business of Government was to divide among them their ill-gotten store. There was no court to which they could be cited, for they themselves filled the bench and composed the juries—there was no tribunal created by public opinion to which virtue could appeal from oppression, or before which profligacy might be arraigned and convicted. No! for there was no press but that worked by the hireling of corruption; or if another press only breathed on gilded or ermined crime, it was subdued, prosecuted, persecuted, and extinguished.*

Such was, unhappily, the system of government established during the years of Irish legislative independence which Grattan achieved for his country. 'I rocked her cradle; I followed her hearse,' said the patriot orator. But the death of this rickety infant need not have caused him any sorrow.

The matter to be lamented was, that, by the unwise and narrow policy of the volunteers, the legislative independence of Ireland was confined to Protestants only; that, in the whole course of imperial policy, government by corruption was substituted for government by force; that at the Union the large and wise plans of Mr. Pitt were rejected, and the miserable monopolising minority had complete sway, dominion, and office, with the short interval of 1806, till 1830.

To overthrow this vicious scheme of administration was the first duty of a liberal Government.

With regard to the Church, the majority of Lord Grey's Cabinet were favourable to the appointment of a commission, by whose inquiries the proportion of the different religious communities could be ascertained, and the ground thus cleared for the erection

* See Godkin's *Ireland and her Churches*, pp. 595–6.

of a superstructure, founded on what was justly due
to Episcopalians, Presbyterians, and Roman Catholics.
The minority of the Cabinet, consisting of Lord
Stanley, Sir James Graham, the Duke of Richmond,
and the Earl of Ripon, dissented from this proposal,
and left the Government of Lord Grey. Soon afterwards a fresh dissension arose, on the question of the
renewal of the Coercion Act; Lord Grey's Government was broken up, and Lord Melbourne, at the
King's request, took the lead in the renewed Administration. Lord Duncannon, who, although he was
not a member of the Cabinet, was on terms of entire
confidence with the leading ministers, was at this
time in correspondence with the King. In one, or
more than one, of his letters, he shadowed forth the
proposal to divert from the purposes of the Protestant Establishment part of the revenues of the Irish
Church. This prospect alarmed to a great degree the
royal mind, so that, when Lord Spencer died, in Nov.
1834, Lord Melbourne received from the King a
letter of dismissal for himself and his colleagues. This
course was premature and unfortunate. The country
could not understand or approve the abrupt banish-
ment from the King's councils of the Ministers who
had carried the Reform Bill. Sir Robert Peel, who
had not been consulted, and who had been brought
from Rome, unwillingly, could not obtain by a disso-
lution and general election a majority for his ministry.
He was defeated on an amendment to the address;
defeated on the London University; defeated on
almost every division, and it soon became evident

that he could not hope to obtain that degree of support from the House of Commons which is necessary for a constitutional minister.

Being defeated on the Irish Church he resigned, and Lord Melbourne resumed his position at the head of the King's Ministry. In 1835, 1836 and 1837, the Appropriation Clause, as it was called, was carried in the House of Commons; but the measure was always rejected by the House of Lords, and Lord Melbourne's Government consented in 1838 to carry the Tithe Measure, without the Appropriation Clause.

It was then made matter of reproach to Lord Melbourne, that as Sir Robert Peel had resigned on the Appropriation Clause, he, Lord Melbourne, had yielded this point, and not resigned his office. But as Sir Robert Peel had never possessed the confidence to obtain which he had dissolved the House of Commons; as the liberal Irish members had complete confidence in Lord Melbourne's Government; as the proposal of the Ministry on the Irish Church went somewhat too far for the English mind, and not nearly far enough to extinguish the Irish grievances, it seemed, upon the whole, to Lord Melbourne and his colleagues that we should only do mischief to Ireland by tendering our resignation.

This may still be a matter for controversy and party taunts.

But at the time the whole question was brought before the House of Commons by me, as the leader of the Government in that House. I moved on April 15, 1839:—

That it is the opinion of this House that it is expedient to persevere in the principles which have guided the Executive Government of Ireland of late years, and which have tended to the effectual administration of the law, and the general improvement of that part of the United Kingdom.

Sir Robert Peel proposed an amendment, and in a very able speech vindicated the course of the Opposition.   The result, after five nights of very animated debate, was that there appeared—

For the amendment	296
For the original motion	318
Majority	22

In the majority were all the liberal members for Ireland: two O'Briens, five O'Connells, the O'Conor Don, Mr. More O'Ferral, Mr. Sheil, and others; all the leading members of the Liberal party, Lord Palmerston, Lord Howick, Sir John Hobhouse, Mr. Labouchere, Lord Morpeth, Mr. Spring Rice, Mr. Charles Wood, Mr. Ellice, and many others.

Such was the deliberate resolution of the party which then governed, and of the Irish Liberals, who were chiefly concerned in supporting the Appropriation Clause.

In this debate I quoted the opinion of Mr. Burke, as given in 1797.   Speaking of the improvement in the laws, he said:—

But the most favourable laws can do very little towards the happiness of a people when the disposition of the ruling power is adverse to them.   Men do not live upon blotted paper. The favourable or the hostile mind of the ruling power is of far more importance to mankind, for good or evil, than the black letter of any statute.

In fact, the Administration of Lord Normanby, Lord Morpeth, and, perhaps more than both, of Thomas . Drummond, the Under-Secretary, was of more value to Ireland than the Appropriation Clause. The mere announcement that property had its duties as well as its rights was a knell to the old Orange Ascendancy, from which that mischievous faction has never recovered. Sir Robert Peel could not, in spite of all his liberality, separate himself from the minority of the Irish people, and from their offensive presumption that the entire government of Ireland belonged to them. When he said that Ireland was his difficulty, he knew well that no Irish Catholic would accept office under him. Unfortunately he had, early in his political life, filled the office of Irish Secretary at a time when Protestant Ascendancy was the motto, the spirit, and the cry of the governing party. When Chief Secretary he adopted that cry. To have changed this cry for that of ' Justice to Ireland,' was the claim of Lord Melbourne to public confidence. The Irish Liberals freely gave that confidence. In fact, the whole spirit of the Irish administration was changed, and the miserable monopolising minority have never been able to restore their *magnum latrocinium.*

We now arrive, then, at the great question of the Irish Established Church. But here, as in other cases, it is well to know the facts before we pronounce an opinion.

Personally the clergy of the Protestant Episcopal

E

Church are now what they were described by Dean Swift to be in his time—namely, country gentlemen in black coats.   But they are much better men than they were in his time.   Dr. Fitzgerald, the present Bishop of Killaloe, has thus described them :—

Of all holders of property in Ireland, since we got rid of the odious old tithe system, the ecclesiastical holders of property give least annoyance to the bulk of the people. They are commonly known as, whatever else they may be, intelligent and respectable benevolent gentlemen, who oppress and injure nobody ; kind and sympathising neighbours, and, according to their means, liberal employers and rewarders of local industry.

Let us take this account of the Episcopal Protestant clergy by one of the heads of their own body as an impartial character of the Church of which he is a distinguished ornament.

But let us also take from another representative of the Irish Church what, in his opinion, are the requisites for the clergy of an Established Church :—

There are two principal requisites needful for this purpose.   One is that their national clergy shall include a fair share of the foremost ability and highest education of the country ; and the other is that their independence in thought and action shall not be unduly fettered.*

Now, one should have thought that, for a ' National Clergy ' who profess to be the followers of Christ, the condition that ' the poor shall have the Gospel preached to them,' would be one of the claims of the

* *Essays on the Irish Church,* p. 44.   A fair and able work.

' National Clergy ' of Ireland, as it is the boast of the Established Church in England.

But here, unfortunately for the clergy of the Protestant Established Church, there occur to our minds certain facts which, whatever may be their share of the 'foremost ability' and 'highest education of the country,' and however 'unfettered their independence of thought and action,' are insuperable obstacles to their preaching the Gospel to the poor.

Let us look at these facts.

The population of Ireland may be taken in round numbers at 5,700,000. Of these the members of the Established Church are about 700,000, or one-eighth of the population. In many benefices, and in many more parishes than benefices, this proportion is not nearly reached, and amounts to no more than 5 per cent., 3 per cent., or even 1 per cent. of the population.

Now, as I have already said, the ordinary notion of an Established Church is, that it is a body which gives religious instruction to the people. Such is the Roman Catholic Church in France, in Austria, and in Spain ; such are the Protestant and Roman Catholic Churches in the dominions of the King of Prussia ; such is the Greek Church in Russia.

Let us here consult the calm and judicious historian Hallam, as to the meaning and use of a Church Establishment :—

An ecclesiastical establishment—that is, the endowment and privileges of a particular religious society—can have no advantages (relatively, at least, to the community where it exists) but its tendency to promote in that community good order and virtue, religious knowledge and edification. But to accomplish this end in any satisfactory manner, it must be their church, and not merely that of the Government; *it should exist for the people, and in the people, and with the people.* *

Nay, even one of the most distinguished among the authors of the ' Essays on the Irish Church,' holding, as it were, a brief for the Establishment, is so impressed by what he sees around him that he writes thus :—

The Roman Catholic Church, indeed, has inherent political tendencies, which do not coincide with those of English politics ; but, even in her case, the evil which results from these in favouring disloyalty and disaffection, is as nothing compared with the good which she does in strengthening the fabric of society by enforcing the obligations of moral duty.†

So that, if we could improve and change the current of these political tendencies, we should have the obligations of moral duty enforced among a population of four millions and a half, instead of among seven hundred thousand only, without any admixture of disloyalty and disaffection. Is it not worth while to try the experiment of equality of all religions before we give up the task in despair ? Should we not feel a strong sympathy with any religious body in Europe placed in the situation of the Catholic Church in Ireland ?

These facts have produced a most unfavourable impression on the minds of the most liberal men—

* Hallam, *Const. Hist.* vol. iii. p. 364, 8vo.
† *Essays on the Irish Church,* p. 23.

men of the 'foremost ability' and 'highest education' in England. Let us see what impression they produced on the mind of Lord Macaulay. I take the extract from one of the able essays of Mr. Aubrey de Vere* :—

What panegyric has ever been pronounced on the Churches of England and Scotland which is not a satire on the Church of Ireland? What traveller who comes among us who is not moved to wonder and derision by the Church of Ireland? What foreign writer on British affairs, whether European or American, whether Protestant or Catholic, whether Conservative or Liberal, whether partial to England, or prejudiced against England, ever mentions the Church of Ireland without expressing his amazement that such an Establishment could exist among reasonable men? And those who speak thus of it speak justly. Is there anything else like it? Was there ever anything else like it? The world is full of ecclesiastical establishments, from the White Sea to the Mediterranean; ecclesiastical establishments from the Wolga to the Atlantic; but nowhere the Church of a small minority, enjoying exclusive establishment. Look at America. There you have all forms of Christianity, from Mormonism, if you call Mormonism Christianity, to Romanism. In some places you have the voluntary system. In some you have several religions connected with the State. In some you have the solitary ascendancy of a single Church. But nowhere, from the Arctic Circle to Cape Horn, do you find the Church of a small minority exclusively established. Look around our own empire. We have an Established Church in England: it is the Church of the majority. There is an Established Church in Scotland. When it was set up it was the Church of the majority. A few months ago it was the Church of

* *The Church Establishment in Ireland illustrated exclusively by Protestant Authorities.* 1867.

the majority. I am not sure that, even after the late un-
happy disruption, it is the Church of the minority. In our
colonies the State does much for the support of religion ;
but in no colony, I believe, do we give exclusive support to
the religion of the minority. Nay, even in those parts of
the empire where the great body of the population is
attached to absurd and immoral superstitions, you have not
been guilty of the folly and injustice of calling on them to
pay for a Church which they do not want. We have not
portioned out Bengal and the Carnatic into parishes, and
scattered Christian rectors, with stipends and glebes, among
millions of pagans and Mahometans.*

But some who are not affected by rhetoric may
have their minds influenced by statistics. I extract
therefore from a very instructive and careful volume,
called ' Ireland and her Churches,' by James Godkin,
some passages, showing the proportion of members of
the Established Church to the population in certain
parts of the country, and in certain parishes.

In some of these instances the incomes of the
parochial clergy ('the national clergy' of Dean
Byrne) are given ; the endowments of the religious
guides and teachers of the majority are, in all cases,
Nil.

The first extract relates to the Diocese of Meath.

The Rev. Dr. Brady has published ' A statistical digest,
exhibiting in a tabular form the present state of endowment
and population in the diocese of Meath, compiled from the
latest returns of the Census and Ecclesiastical Commissioners
of Ireland,' from which I extract the following figures :
The number of benefices is 105, composed of 204 parishes,
containing 107 churches, and having 105 incumbents. The

* *Hansard*, vol. lxxix., pp. 1182–5.

gross income of the Sec is 4,308*l.* 2*s.* 3*d.*, the net
3,664*l.* 16*s.* 4*d.* The total gross income of the benefices
is 30,717*l.* 11*s.* 11*d.*, net income 24,504*l.* 4*s.* 4*d.*, giving an
average net income per benefice of 243*l.* 7*s.* 5*d.* If we add
the tithes, disappropriated from the See, and the value of the
deanery lands of Clonmacnoise (1,686*l.* 4*s.* 9*d.*), with the
revenue of the five suspended parishes (475*l.* 7*s.*), the gross
total of the ecclesiastical revenues of Meath will amount to
37,187*l.* The total population of the Established Church,
for which this provision is made, is 15,869, giving 151 souls
for each benefice; the Roman Catholic population being
221,553, or 2,110 souls for each benefice. The diocese con-
tains only 1,865 Dissenters. Without counting the bishop's
income, the endowment per head of the Church population is,
gross, 1*l.* 18*s.* 8*d.* ; net, 1*l.* 10*s.* 10*d.* This is exclusive of
240 persons, who form the Church population of fourteen
impropriate parishes, in which there is no provision for the
cure of souls; and of twenty-nine persons who form the
Church population of five suspended parishes; and of 151
members of the Established Church, who are inmates of
public institutions, whose spiritual wants are otherwise provided for by the State. If these be added, the gross population is 16,289.

The following table relates to the four united
Dioceses of Killaloe, Kilfenora, Clonfert, Kilmacduagh.

Diocese	No. of benefices	Net Income	Average for each Incumbent	Cost per head of Church Population	Total Population	Established Church Population	Proportion of Church Members to entire Population
		£	£	£ s. d.			per cent.
Killaloe	67	14,055	209	1 2 0	225,096	12,700	5
Kilfenora	7	1,416	202	5 12 0	23,042	251	1
Clonfert	13	3,080	237	1 4 0	64,143	2,521	4
Kilmacduagh	4	1,603	400	3 13 0	42,798	434	1
Total for united diocese	91	20,154	221	1 5 0	355,079	15,906	

The next return relates to the united Dioceses of Waterford and Lismore.

Name of Benefice	No. of Parishes	No. of Members of Established Church	Net Income	Total Population
			£	
Killoteran . . .	1	10	116	417
Ballynakill . . .	4	94	182	2,054
Affane	2	93	234	3,505
Modeligo	2	6	135	1,481
Ardmore	2	85	458	4,978
Templemichael . . .	2	65	237	2,071
Lisgenaul	1	13	149	1,223
Rossmire	2	18	183	2,376
Fenough	1	12	145	782
Prebend of Mora . .	1	3	193	414
Mothell	1	27	465	4,312
Kilsheelan . . .	1	21	186	1,435
Derrygrath . . .	1	13	254	757
Lisronagh . . .	1	9	195	519
Outragh	2	10	197	537
Tubrid	3	21	400	4,692
Templetenny . . .	1	3	139	3,967
Ardfinnan . . .	3	42	247	1,320
Total . . .	31	544	4,115	36,870

The Archdeacon of Connor, the Venerable Thomas Hincks, has framed a table showing the contrast between eight denominations of Connor in the north of Ireland, and forty-two benefices selected out of two southern dioceses.

No.	Eight Denominations of Connor. Forty-two Benefices in the South	In eight Denominations of Connor	In forty-two Benefices in two Southern Dioceses
1	Total population amounts to . .	11,163	47,657
2	Number of members of Established Church	1,304	559
3	Average population of each . . .	1,395·3	1,134·7
4	Average number of members of Established Church	163	13·3
5	Percentage of po- { Established Church	11·7	1·2
	pulation . . { Dissenters . .	88·3	98·8
6	Net income of the whole . . .	nil	£6,595 15s.
7	Average net income to each . . .	nil	£157

Let us now pause to consider for a moment the state of facts. The Episcopal Protestant clergymen, we will admit, are learned, kind, charitable, well fitted to be the members of a society of gentlemen of education and property. But, on the other hand, it cannot be denied that not more than an eighth, sometimes a tenth or a twentieth of the population listen to their religious teaching. Surely this is an unsatisfactory state of things.

If, for instance, the Roman Catholic inhabitants of Sweden amounted to only one eighth of the population, but had possession of the whole of the funds allotted by the State to religious instruction, there is no doubt we should wonder at so strange an anomaly, and should heartily sympathise with the Swedish Protestants who claimed a different distribution of the Church revenues.

But what is the obstacle ? Let us first listen to Lord Cairns, who would stop us *in limine* with an insuperable objection to an appropriation of the revenues of the Protestant Church of Ireland to any other Church or any secular purpose. After speaking of the Act of Settlement of 1662, and the glebe lands, and some parts of the tithe rent charge, Lord Cairns goes on to say, ' With regard to the title of the other portion of the rent-charge, it may well be rested on what in this country has always been considered the best title to any property, the title of prescription.'*
Now, in respect to a settled state of affairs, there can be no doubt that prescription is an excellent title; still, even in a settled state of affairs, there may be exceptions.

* *Hansard*, vol. clxxxviii.   June 24, 1867.

If, for instance, an estate were left to trustees, with an obligation to redeem captives in the custody of the Dey of Algiers, or to give medical care to persons who should return from the Holy Land afflicted with leprosy, and to apply the rest of the revenue to their own enjoyment, Parliament would hardly consider that, if there were no captives in Algiers, and no pilgrims afflicted with leprosy, the whole income would be rightly applied as if it were the private estate of the trustees. But let us again listen to Lord Cairns. In speaking of a title to ecclesiastical property, Lord Cairns says :—

In the hottest debates on that subject there was always one point which every person admitted, and is quite sufficient for my present purpose. It was always admitted that so long as the corporate body which possessed the title to ecclesiastical property remains, so long as the property is not greater in amount than can be usefully applied by that corporate body. . . . there is no right of principle on which Parliament can interfere to alienate property of that kind.*

But this case is not only modified, it is entirely altered, if the nation has changed its views in regard to the application of funds. Supposing William of Wykeham had founded a public college at Oxford, on the condition that the monks or scholars should pray for his soul, and sing mattins, the statesmen and legislators of Elizabeth would not have thought themselves precluded from a different appropriation of the funds, even were the masses rightly performed, and the mattins and vespers regularly celebrated.

* *Hansard*, vol. clxxxviii.   June 24, 1867.

In fact, the ecclesiastical tithes, and the rent-charges for which they were commuted, the Church lands, and the large estates of bishops, chapters, and colleges, have all been appropriated in violation of that law of prescription to which Lord Cairns so confidently appeals. The conduct of the clergy, that is, of the secular clergy, was not in violation of their trusts, but the mind and the policy of the nation had changed. By the Acts of Supremacy and Uniformity, passed in the beginning of the reign of Queen Elizabeth, England was finally separated from Rome, and all persons having ecclesiastical dignities or cure of souls were bound to conform to the Reformed Church. Burnet and Strype tell us that, according to the reports of visitors appointed by the Queen, only about one hundred dignitaries and eighty parish priests refused to accept the Protestant formularies, and resigned or were deprived of their benefices. Burnet says pensions were reserved for those who quitted their benefices on account of religion; and the historian Hallam, far from exclaiming against the expulsion of Roman Catholic dignitaries and parish priests on account of their religion, praises the grant of pensions as 'a very liberal measure.' It may be said indeed that on this great occasion the whole nation changed and the government with them.

The case of Scotland, however, approaches much nearer that which now presents itself in regard to Ireland. In 1688 England had endeavoured for many years to establish Episcopacy in Scotland, against the will of its people. England was by no means dis-

posed at that time to renounce Episcopacy : William
the Third preferred it to the Presbyterian form of
Church Government.   Indeed, the Confession of Westminster had been a kind of symbol of the majority of
the Republican party in the reign of Charles the First,
and the Presbyterians had divided with the Inde-
pendents the Church and the Universities during the
Commonwealth.

These were strong motives with King William and
his English councillors for refusing to abolish Episcopacy in Scotland in 1688.   But the Scotch nation
would take no denial.   They made it one of the
articles in their Declaration of Rights that prelacy
and precedence in ecclesiastical offices were repug-
nant to the genius of a nation reformed by presbyters,
and an insupportable grievance which ought to be
abolished.*   William yielded, and Episcopacy was
abolished.   There is a passage in 'Hallam' upon this
subject so characteristic and so instructive that I
cannot refrain from quoting it :—

The main controversy between the Episcopal and Presbyterian Churches was one of historical inquiry, not perhaps
capable of decisive solution ; it was at least one as to which
the bulk of mankind are absolutely incapable of forming a
rational judgment for themselves ; but mingled up as it
had always been, and most of all in Scotland, with faction,
with revolution, with power and emolument, with courage
and devotion, and fear, and hate, and revenge, this dispute
drew along with it the most glowing devotions of the heart,
and the question became utterly out of the province of argument.   It is very possible that episcopacy might be of
apostolical institution ; but for this institution houses had been

* Hallam's *Const. Hist.* vol. iii. p. 320.

burned, and fields laid waste, and the Gospel had been preached in wildernesses, and its ministers had been shot in their prayers, and husbands had been murdered before their wives, and virgins had been defiled, and many had died by the executioner, and by massacre, and in imprisonment, and in exile, and slavery, and women had been tied to stakes on the sea-shore till the tide rose to overflow them, and some had been tortured and mutilated; it was a religion of the boots and the thumb-screw, which a good man must be very cool-blooded indeed if he did not hate and reject from the hands which offered it. For, after all, it is much more certain that the Supreme Being abhors cruelty and persecution, than that He has set up bishops to have a superiority over presbyters.*

I give this passage, firstly, to impress upon you and my readers the memorable and gratifying fact that, in spite of all these oppressions and cruelties, Scotland is now a contented and flourishing part of the United Kingdom ; partly to inculcate the lesson that this marvellous change was effected by the sacrifice of the Episcopal Church of Scotland. Macaulay tells us how the Episcopal clergy were rabbled, that is to say, their houses were sacked, and they with their families driven away ; and Hallam records that, owing to the love of religious freedom of William, some of these clergymen returned, and were allowed to reside in their old benefices. But no one can deny that Episcopacy was dis-established, and that Presbytery was set up in its place. Nor will any one contend that the English sovereign or the English people preferred the Westminster Confession of Faith and Presbytery to the Episcopal Church of England, any more

* *Hallam*, vol. iii. p. 329.

than they now prefer Cardinal Cullen to Archbishop
Trench, or Maynooth to Oxford.   But they thought
the Church of the people of Scotland ought to be the
Church of the State in Scotland.

Having thus shown that, in two leading examples,
the clergy were deprived of their property, although
they fully complied with the conditions on which they
had received it, I affirm, without hesitation, that the
Protestant Established Church of Ireland is the main
grievance of which the people have to complain ; that
the Roman Catholic clergy and their flocks are alike
dissatisfied ; that the present state of Church Endowment would not be borne in any country of Europe;
and I proceed to consider the remedies which can be
applied to this diseased state of the body politic.

And here, in the first place, I discard my own
remedy of 1835.   I believe the Appropriation Clause
would, if adopted at the time, have given satisfaction
to the Irish people, and have afforded a breathing
time for the consideration of later and larger measures.

But that proposal was rejected by Parliament, and
I am the first to say that what would have been
healing in 1835 would be futile in 1868.

Instead, therefore, of resorting to the partial
remedy of 1835, I will consider the proposal of the
Liberation Society, who, according to Lord Cairns,
are at the bottom of all the agitation about the Irish
Church.

It must be admitted that the Liberation Society
have a large principle upon which they found their
proposals.

They say, as O'Connell used to say, Let every man send for his own priest as every man sends for his own doctor. But I have no intention to discuss with the Liberation Society the mighty question involved in the voluntary principle. All I say on behalf of myself, and of those who, like myself, have a prejudice in favour of Church Establishments, is this, 'If you seek to re-constitute society in the United Kingdom on a new principle, do not satisfy yourselves with attacking the wall where it is weakest; do not give us your revolution in driblets; let us consider the whole breadth of your proposed change —above all, do not forget altogether what is good for Ireland while you are seeking to emancipate mankind.' Yet to this point they seem to have paid little attention. Accordingly, at their last meeting, after unanimously sweeping away the funds of the Irish Church, their members fell into all kinds of discordant proposals as to the application of these funds, some one or two, not reflecting that the landlords are amply paid for collecting the tithe rent-charge by a commission of 25 per cent., were for offering the other 75 per cent. as a bribe to their cupidity.

Let us, however, look at the question somewhat more modestly and somewhat more practically.

The Roman Catholic farmer is heavily taxed for his Church. The churches themselves, which used to be

Such humble roofs as piety can raise,

have of late years, instead of mere tenements of wood, become handsome buildings of stone, with the appropriate ornaments. A Roman Catholic Bishop told me that he had required a rate of five shillings in the pound on the valuation of a parish for the erection of one of these churches. The priest has often 200*l.* a year, and his curate 100*l.* In some places the Catholic rector has 500*l.* a year. The fee for a marriage is often 15*l.* or 20*l.* The Liberation Society propose to leave the Catholic farmer and the Catholic peasant subject to all these exactions, but in compensation the Protestant rector is to disappear. The farmer will find no demand for his eggs and butter from a resident Protestant clergyman; the peasant will have no charitable assistance from the wife and daughters of the clergyman. What will be the result? The voluntary, or rather necessary, payments of the Catholic farmer will continue; the purchases in the market and the alms in the hand of the country gentleman in a black coat will cease.

The balance can only be a considerable loss. Yet if we decline to adopt this plan, we must not suppose that the existing evil would be remedied were the revenues of the southern benefices carried over to Down, Armagh, and Antrim. Let us hear Sir George Lewis on such partial reforms :—

The true ground of complaint is that the State, having a certain endowment for ecclesiastical purposes at its disposal, selects one religious persuasion as the object of its favour, and that one the persuasion of only a tenth part of the community. It is ever to be remembered, in discussing the ecclesiastical state of Ireland, that the objections of the Roman Catholics to the Established Church of that country, are not of *more* or *less*; that they would not be removed by the abolition of a few bishoprics, or the paring down of a few benefices, but that they lie against its very existence; against the principle of making a public provision in Ireland for the clergy of the small minority, so long as the clergy of the large majority is left wholly destitute of aid from the public funds. No improvements in the internal economy of the Established Church, in the distribution of its revenues, or the discipline of its clergy, tend to lessen the sense of grievance arising from this source. The effect of the preference in question is that the whole body of the Catholics in Ireland are *more or less alienated from the Government*— the author of their wrong—and are filled with jealousy and ill-will towards the more favoured Protestants. . . . All the ecclesiastical grievances of Ireland arise from what is termed the connexion between Church and State, which gives to our ecclesiastical society *exclusive civil rights and privileges.* The great principle which ought to serve as the basis of legislation in all ecclesiastical matters, is that *the State is no judge of the truth of creeds.* In proportion as this principle has been violated, all ecclesiastical legislation has been mischievous and oppressive.[*]

There can be no doubt that, if we were to hear of such a state of things in a foreign country, we should sympathise with those who were ' more or less alienated from the Government.'

But if six-eighths of the tithe rent-charge were employed in building churches, in purchasing glebes and glebe houses for the Catholic clergy, and furnishing a better income to the poorer ministers of the Catholic Church, some 300,000*l.* a year would be saved to the Irish farmer, and he would then willingly submit to the loss of the custom and the charity of

---

[*] *Irish Disturbances and the Irish Church Question,* p. 341.

the Protestant rector.   The priest would then diffuse
in his parish the religious instruction which, at the
expense of the State, he had imbibed at Maynooth.

I am not arguing, you will observe, on the large
principles which would leave every religious community to be supported by voluntary contributions;
I am only giving my own opinion as an individual,
that the destruction of the Protestant Church in
Ireland, the withdrawal of the Grant to Maynooth,
and of the *Regium Donum* to the Presbyterians of
the North, together with a refusal of all subsidies by
the State towards the building of Roman Catholic
churches, and furnishing glebes and incomes to the
Catholic clergy, would be a misfortune for Ireland.
It would manifestly check civilisation, and arrest the
progress of society in the rural parts of Ireland.   If
given to education, it would deprive Ireland of large
grants which now flow from the Imperial Exchequer.
So, likewise, if the revenues were applied to public
works.   I, therefore, come to the conclusion, that the
endowment of the Roman Catholic Church in Ireland,
the endowment of the Presbyterian Church, and the
reduction of the Protestant Episcopal Church to one-
eighth of the present Church Revenues of Ireland,
would be just and salutary.

I come now to consider the objections which may
be made by persons who, admitting the right of the
State to deal with the property assigned to the Protestant Episcopal Church, would yet resist on various
grounds the adoption of such a scheme as that of
which I have given a rough sketch.

We may suppose the first objection to be on the part of Conservatives in both Houses of Parliament, who would say—'There is already a Commission appointed on your own motion. Wait till they have made their inquiries, and suggested in their Report the remedial measures which they consider appropriate to the case. This is surely a reasonable request.' I should admit the request to be reasonable if the whole case of the churches existing in Ireland had been submitted for inquiry to commissioners fit for the task, and they had been left at liberty to consider what was best for the welfare of the Irish people.

But this last question is expressly excluded from the inquiries and report of the Commission. Fearing that this might be the case, I added to my motion for an inquiry 'into the amount and nature of the property and resources of the Established Church in Ireland, and as to the means of rendering that property more productive,' the words 'and to their more equitable application for the benefit of the Irish people.'

But the very idea of the benefit of the Irish people being left as an open question to be considered by the Commissioners, alarmed the Government and the Irish Bishops. They struck out 'the benefit of the Irish people' altogether, and confined the inquiry to the questions of rendering the property more productive, and, if I rightly interpret the terms of the Commission, into the propriety of a better distribution of the funds of the Established Church. Now, in my view, an inquiry into the means of rendering the property

more productive, excluding any regard to its more
equitable application for the benefit of the Irish people,
would be quite unsatisfactory and quite useless.   But
if it is contemplated—as the present Primate of Ireland once contemplated—to have fewer clergymen
and larger unions in the South and West of Ireland,
and to transfer the revenues thus procured to benefices in the North, where the Protestant congregations
are considerable, I must say that, in the view of the
' benefit of the Irish people,' such a transfer would be
positively mischievous.

The best character an Irish Protestant clergyman
can assume, that which Dean Swift gave him in
the last century and which the Bishop of Killaloe
gives him in the present, is that of a resident country
gentleman in a black coat.

But if you carry away this resident country gentleman from counties where the revenue accrues, where
country gentlemen are scarce, and the example of a
man of education conversant with justice, and of his
family conversant with charity, is really useful, and
divert his income derived from the parish or parishes
in his neighbourhood to another parish or parishes in
a distant county, in order to relieve the great lords
and rich propri.tors of the north from the obligation
of augmenting, out of their own pockets, the means of
clergymen who give spiritual instruction to their neigh-
bours in Armagh, in Antrim, and in Down, you will
heighten the injustice and aggravate the evils of the
Irish Church established by law.

But, say some sanguine persons, the Reformation

may still prosper in Ireland. The Protestant clergy are more generally resident and more fully instructed than they ever were before ; let us wait and see the effects of their labours in the vineyard before we pluck up by the roots our budding plants. Sanguine persons indeed ! The Roman Catholic Church has withstood in Europe and in Ireland the fiercest storms. In France it has survived Voltaire and Lepaux, the French Revolution and the Goddess of Reason ; in England, Queen Elizabeth, William the Third, and the Penal Laws. In Ireland it still confronts us with four times as many adherents as all the Protestant churches. If we look to the fate of sovereigns, we find that James the Second forfeited the crown of England, and that Charles the Tenth sacrificed the crown of France, rather from devotion to the Church of Rome than from the failure of their political ambition. If we enquire among the learned, we find in England Dr. Manning and Mr. Newman quitting the Protestant for the Catholic Church ; in France, Montalembert giving his thrilling eloquence in behalf of the infallible Pope. If we look for examples of domestic purity, and the devotion of every faculty to religion, we find examples in the highest Catholic families of France.*

But has the Reformation no chance in Ireland ?

A fair chance, I should say, but not by means of the mitres and privileged seats in the House of Lords. As in large towns the first Christian apostles and teachers converted the Gentiles, in spite of Nero, of

* See especially the two affecting volumes entitled *Récit d'une Sœur.*

Trajan, of Diocletian, so in large towns in Ireland, Protestant preachers, earnest and eloquent, are even now collecting numerous congregations, aided by no endowment, filling their chapels to the brim, and eloquently unfolding to their hearers the whole counsel of God.

If the Established Church is cut down to the proportions which befit it, we may expect to see reformers occupy the positions of Polycarp and of Cyprian,

> And by persuasion do the work of fear.

If Protestants believe, as I think they do, in the justice of their opposition to Rome, let them grant to the Roman Church equal arms, and fight, as Luther and Zuinglius fought, with argument and with zeal, exposing the abuses of the Church against which they protest. Let us not, therefore, while we do justice to Catholics, give up the title of Protestants for ourselves.

It is next said that it would be wrong to endow a religion which is not the religion of the State. And is the Church of Scotland the religion of the State? Is Maynooth a Protestant institution? But what says Dr. Johnson on this head ?

> For my part, sir, I think all Christians, whether Papists or Protestants, agree in the essential articles, and that their differences are trivial, and rather political than religious.*

So likewise John Wesley, while a most decided Protestant, would not allow it to be said that a relation of his, from having joined the Roman Catholic Church, had thereby changed his religion. He ad-

---

* Boswell's *Johnson*, vol. i. p. 374.

mitted errors in the Catholic Church, but said that religion was quite a different thing, and that his relation might still retain his allegiance to Christ. In fact, the Roman Catholics form a great majority of the Catholic Church.

The next objection comes from a very different quarter. The Irish Roman Catholic Bishops, with Cardinal Cullen at their head, have at a solemn meeting in the month of October last agreed to two resolutions. The one affirms in substance that the revenues of the Church (whatever they may be) belong to the Roman Catholic Church. The other affirms in substance that the Roman Catholic Church will not accept any pecuniary assistance from the Government of the United Kingdom. My first impression on reading these resolutions was a recollection of a story in Spanish biography. It is related of Gonsalvo de Cordova, called the Gran Capitan by his countrymen, that he was promised by King Ferdinand the high post of Grand Master of the Order of Calatrava. But the King having afterwards altered his mind, and disposed of the post otherwise, sent to the Great Captain to offer him the city of Loja. ‘ No ! ’ said Don Gonsalvo; ‘ tell the King that I prefer my grievance to the city of Loja.’

Such seems to be the disposition of the Roman Catholic Bishops of Ireland. They prefer their grievance to a grant from the Imperial Treasury. For, be it observed, they keep in reserve, even in the case of the abolition of the Irish Church Establishment, their claims for the property of the Roman Catholic Church as it existed before the Reformation. This claim therefore would still remain, and when the voluntary principle had been fully established in Ireland, would be put forward as the perpetual ever-lasting grievance of the Irish priests and people.

Let us remark also upon this subject, that the nine-teenth century has seen a strange and unexpected, but very powerful, effort of the clerical body in France, in Belgium, and in the United Kingdom, to place the ecclesiastical element above the civil.

In Scotland we have seen an attempt made by the ablest members of the Scotch Church to set aside the authority of an Act of Parliament, an attempt which enlisted many liberal men in its favour, and which it required all the ability of Sir William Follett, and the weight of a majority in Parliament, to resist. In England we are now witnesses of an endeavour on the part of certain ecclesiastics, very highly placed, to establish sacerdotal rule in place of that supremacy of the civil power which three cen-turies ago Henry the Eighth induced Parliament to substitute for the appeal to Rome. And can we ex-pect that an ecclesiastical sovereign, strong in the traditions of emperors holding the Pope's stirrup and humbly acknowledging their transgressions at Rome and at Venice ; strong in records of a Queen of Eng-land deposed, and a King of France excommunicated, and whose maxim is *Vestigia nulla retrorsum,* should not cling to old pretensions, and endeavour to make all the Queen's subjects acknowledge the right of the Pope to exercise jurisdiction and authority in these kingdoms ?

Our only resource is to maintain the supremacy of Parliament as the great lay tribunal. 'L'État est Laïc,' as M. Guizot once said of France. The Queen's title must be upheld, her Courts of Justice must not be subject to appeal to Scotch Presbyteries, or Pan-Anglican Synods, or Roman tribunals.

But there is in all this nothing to prevent the settlement of Church property in Ireland now held by the Protestant clergy in an equitable manner. The Irish Catholic bishops may resist; but the Irish Catholic farmer, and the Irish Catholic cottier, aye, and the Roman Catholic parish priest, will rejoice in such a settlement. The half-voluntary half-compulsory payments will be diminished, and Parliament will have consulted, what the House of Lords erased from my proposed resolution, 'the benefit of the Irish people.'

Yet, while applying certain revenues to the purposes of the Roman Catholic Church, we must beware of falling into an error which has already cost us dear. Mr. Pitt, it is evident, had it in contemplation to clip that independence of the Roman Catholic Church in Ireland which forms the security of that Church against interference by the State. Lord Grenville and even Mr. Grattan kept this object in view. In 1825, when a grant from the public funds for the support of the Roman Catholic clergy was in contemplation, Lord Liverpool, in discussion with his friends, objected to the words, 'that provision should be made *by law*.' He had evidently the same notion in his head which Mr. Pitt had clearly avowed.

The Roman Catholic clergy rightly object to any notion of the sort. A salary voted by Parliament like the old grant to Maynooth and the present *Regium Donum*, and liable, therefore, to be withheld on the motion of a Mr. —— or Mr. ——, would be most objectionable. It would embarrass the Catholic clergy, unwilling as they would be, to surrender any portion of their independence, but at the same time reluctant to throw up a public provision and recur again to the charity of their flocks. In order to give security to the Catholics and permanence to the settlement of Ireland, it would be necessary that the sums to be applied to the purposes of the Catholic Church should be placed to their credit, and be at the disposal, on conditions laid down by Parliament, of persons chosen in the same manner as the Catholic portion of Sir R. Peel's Board for Charitable Bequests. That portion consists of the Chief Baron, being at present a Catholic, and five other Roman Catholic members. Such a board should have power to appropriate the funds:—

1. To build or repair Catholic churches.

2. To furnish glebe houses and glebe lands to parish priests.

The sum set apart to furnish or augment the incomes of parish priests might, according to a suggestion of Mr. O'Connell in 1825, be placed in provincial banks, to be drawn out by them at their own convenience.

Bishop Doyle, whose name ought never to be mentioned without a tribute of respect and admiration,

was not averse to a provision to be made by Parliament for objects in which assistance to the clergy was
included. He proposed that tithes should be utterly
abolished, the Church lands transferred, and a land-
tax of one-tenth of the produce of the land substituted for tithes. The objects to be aimed at were,
'to provide amply for the support of the poor; *to
assist when necessary the ministers of religion*; to
educate all the people; and to promote to the greatest
possible extent works of public necessity or national
improvement.'

This is too vague and too wide a scheme to be now
adopted; tithes have, since that time, been commuted
for rent-charges, and education has been in a great
degree assisted by Parliamentary votes. The abolition of the tithe rent-charge would give no satisfaction; the imposition of a land-tax on Ireland in place
of a grant from the Imperial Revenue would cause
discontent.

Another objection to such a scheme as has been
here suggested is founded on the misuse of a word.
It is said to be absurd to have three Church Establishments in Ireland. But Sir George Lewis, in speaking
of the Protestant and Roman Catholic Churches in
Prussia, has truly said:—

'Arguments against religious establishments are
not, therefore, arguments against religious endowments.'

There is, indeed, one facility in Prussia which we
have not here. The Protestants in Prussia have no
bishops. The Pope consented to abolish the Arch-

bishopric of Aix-la-Chapelle, and the King consented to acknowledge the Archbishop of Cologne.

Our best course in the United Kingdom is rather to rely on our own Statutes and those of our ancestors, both before and since the Reformation, than to embarrass ourselves in negotiations with the Pope.

Some persons, entertaining a very natural sense of the disinclination of the English people to large measures, are of opinion that it would be enough to propose a clipping of the wings of the Established Church in Ireland, and a provision out of her surplus funds for glebe lands and churches for the Roman Catholics in that country.

But it seems to me that any such half measure, leaving Protestant Ascendancy in full blowing dignity, would not suit the present time. The moment has arrived for equality to be granted or denied. Halting between two opinions will satisfy no party.

I come now, therefore, to what is asked by the Lay Peers and Members of the House of Commons of the Roman Catholic faith. Let us first remark who these are. They belong to the class who have derived the greatest benefit from the Relief Act of 1829. They have been enabled by that Act to bear their part, and exercise their functions in the Legislation of the country. Among them are to be found lawyers who may aspire to the highest ranks of their profession. They now come forward to ask for their humbler countrymen—the priests sprung from the middle classes, the farmers and peasants of their faith—those advantages which are justly their due.

They do not ask, like the Scotch Parliament of
1690, to acquire exclusive privileges for their own
Church; they do not, like the Scotch of 1697, propose
that the Protestant Episcopal Church of England
should be accounted in Ireland a Dissenting sect,
while their own Church is Established; what they
ask is, that the four millions and a half of Roman
Catholics should be placed on an equality with the
700,000 Protestants of the Episcopal Church.

Surely there is nothing arrogant, nothing defying,
nothing seditious or revolutionary in this request.

It says, in effect, to the Parliament of the United
Kingdom—If in your wisdom you think it right to
abolish Church Endowments, let us have the benefit
of that principle; if, on the other hand, you decide to
maintain Church Endowments, let the principle of
Equality obtain for our faith, in the revenues set
apart for this purpose by the State, that share to
which our population justly entitles us.

I will now, therefore, state roughly the consequences
of adopting the principle of Equality in regard to the
three Churches of Ireland.

In the first place the Protestant Episcopal Church
would cease to be an Established Church. Established Churches are immediately and closely connected
with the State; Endowed Churches only acknowledge
the State as the Power by whose authority they receive their revenues. The Protestant Episcopal
Church in Ireland, therefore, in ceasing to be Established, would cease to have its archbishops and bishops
sitting in the House of Lords; Parliament might pro-

vide for the number of bishops to be maintained, and
the mode of their election or appointment: those
bishops would have no precedence, they would be,
like The Most Rev. Archbishop Crolly and The Right
Rev. Bishop Denvir,* known only to the Secretary of
State and the ' London Gazette ' by their names, and
not by their jurisdictions.   To the members of their
own Church each would assume his ecclesiastical title;
Archbishop Trench would be Archbishop of Dublin
to his own communion; Archbishop Cullen would
assume a similar title in addressing the faithful of his.
own Church.

A fair division of the rent-charge in lieu of tithes
would give about six-eighths to the Roman Catholic,
about one-eighth to the Protestant Episcopal, and less
than an eighth to the Presbyterian Church.

Questions would no doubt arise respecting the property in glebe lands.   Lord Cairns contends that many
of these glebe lands were forfeited to the State, and
were granted to the Protestant Church by the Act of
1662.   Mr. Hallam remarks that many of these lands
had belonged to the Church, and had fallen into lay
hands during the confusion of the Civil War.   These
are questions for Commissions to investigate in the
first instance, and for Parliament in the last resort to
decide.

On the subject of Education, I shall content myself
with very few words.   The plan at present in opera-
tion was devised by Lord Monteagle; it was put in

* *London Gazette*, 1845.

force by Lord Derby. It is religious, but unsectarian; it affords the best secular instruction, and is within the reach, omitting headlands and islands, of every boy and girl in Ireland. The Queen, in visiting the Model School in Dublin, says: ' From here we drove to the Model School, where we were received by the Archbishop of Dublin, the Roman Catholic Archbishop Murray (a fine venerable-looking old man of eighty), and the other gentlemen connected with the school. . . . . Children of all creeds are admitted, and their different doctrines are taught separately, if the parents wish it; but the *only* teaching enforced is that of the Gospel truths, and love and charity. This is truly Christian, and ought to be the case everywhere.'* I have only to add to this sentiment a fervent, Amen.

* *Leaves from the Journal of our Life in the Highlands from* 1848 *to* 1861, p. 257. Edited by Arthur Helps.

PART III.

I HAVE now given an outline of the history of the
Imperial Policy towards Ireland for the last forty
years, of the grievances which yet remain—the
broken links of a chain which galled the Irish people
for more than two centuries—and of the remedial
measures which, in my opinion, are still required to
give to Ireland the equality promised by Mr. Pitt
when he gave her the semblance of a union with
Great Britain.

But there are two things required to carry measures, even of the utmost importance and the greatest
public benefit, in Parliament.   The one of these is a
tide of public opinion sufficiently strong to bear along
with it to the ocean of oblivion the old prejudices,
the traditional stock of arguments, and the private
interests which block up the river, and convert the
wholesome current of legislation into a stagnant pool.
The other requisite is a man or men fit to take the
lead—to direct the course to be pursued in Parliament, to digest the information received, and to frame
the measures to be recommended.

In regard to the first requisite, it may be remarked,
that public opinion in this country is apt to be long
quiescent and suddenly impetuous.   From 1820 to
1830, there was scarcely any apparent movement on

the subject of Reform. In 1830–31 there was not only movement, but agitation, disturbance, riot. From 1860 to 1866 there was again repose. In 1866 there was a loud demand for further reforms; so much so, that the strongest adversaries of moderate change became the most eager advocates of ill-considered innovation.

With respect to Ireland, the opinion of England has never yet been in a very active or very satisfactory state. The Relief Act of 1829 was acquiesced in as a necessity: it was clear that no leading man in Parliament, neither the Duke of Wellington nor Lord Grey, neither Mr. Peel nor Mr. Brougham, would have undertaken to carry on the Government on any other terms. The Appropriation Clause of 1835 was never heartily approved by the English people, and the cry of ' No Popery!' was raised with some success against it. Since that measure was given up, apathy has prevailed. But now a feeling has arisen favourable to the settlement of the Irish question. It is felt in earnest that Ireland is not treated by England as any other country in Europe is treated by its metropolitan state, and that, in case of a foreign war, at least half our army will be required to garrison Ireland. It is said, indeed, that we have made no concessions to Ireland, except from fear. The reproach is not undeserved. But that reflection need not deter our legislators. King John did not sign Magna Charta from pure benevolence, nor did Charles the Second and his brother, the Duke of York, consent to the Habeas

Corpus Act without reluctance.*   Nor did the great
Tory party consent to Catholic Emancipation, except
from fear, or embrace Household Suffrage, until the
railings of Hyde Park had been levelled to the
ground, and sundry meetings had taken place, more
remarkable for their numbers and their physical
force than for argment or for eloquence.   Such re-
proaches may induce us to regret past injustice, but
must not deter our Parliament from doing justice—
now late, indeed, but not too late.   So that the old
plan of governing Ireland by a corrupt cabal having
been abandoned, and the will of the people of England
being generally in favour of ecclesiastical equality in
Ireland, we may hope that the Irish Church will not
be much longer an obstacle to peace.   But men also
are required to effect this mighty and beneficial revolution.   Mr. Canning, following on this subject the
doctrines of Fox, said most truly, ' Away with the
cant of measures, not men—the idle supposition, that
it is the harness, and not the horses, that draws the
chariot along.'

For the great task of pacifying Ireland, by just
and righteous measures, a man is required, not affected with the weakness of age, but vigorous with
the strength of manhood, having a seat in the House
of Commons, and possessing its confidence.

Mr. Canning possessed that confidence from the
power of his oratory, and the generosity of his foreign
policy.

Lord Althorp possessed that confidence, not from

* See *Memoirs of James the Second.*

his eloquence as an orator, for he was no orator, but from his transparent honesty and liberal principles. When Lord Grey had obtained from the King sufficient security for carrying the Reform Bill, Lord Althorp said, ' I feel a full assurance that we can carry the Reform Bill in its integrity. I cannot give you the grounds of that assurance, but I trust the House has sufficient confidence in me to accept my word.' When Lord Althorp arrived at the words ' confidence in me,' there was such a shout in the House of Commons, as I never heard before or since.

If, then, we can find a man with the brilliant oratory of Canning, and the sterling honesty of Althorp, it is to such a man that the destiny of this country and the prospects of Ireland ought to be consigned.

The University of Oxford, overflowing with bigotry, might indeed reject such a man, but I feel persuaded the great county of Lancaster would never fail him, nor would the country at large cease to celebrate his pure and immortal fame.

What, then, is required to solve this great question of the Irish Church? Is it anything so difficult as to be unattainable? Far from it. Two steps only are required.

The first is a resolution of the House of Commons, affirming the ecclesiastical equality asked for as a boon to Ireland by the most eminent of the Roman Catholic laymen; the other, an address to the Crown, praying for measures to give effect to that resolution. No Ministers of the Crown would advise the Queen to refuse her consideration to this resolution, or try to shuffle it away in a pigeon-hole to be thought of some time next year.

We should thus naturally look in the first instance to the public speeches of the Ministers of the Crown. We shall presently find in the recorded debates of 1844, an emphatic and well-considered declaration of opinion from the present Chancellor of the Exchequer, the leader of the House.

It so happened, that in that year, I moved, on February 13, for a Committee of the whole House to consider the state of Ireland. In speaking of the Church, I said :—

For my own part, I do not think you can remove the grievances which now press upon Ireland, unless, on the one hand, by adopting the voluntary principle, or, on the other, by making an Establishment not for one, but for all religions which exist there. With respect to the voluntary principle, I think that it is liable to insuperable objections.

After arguing that point, I said :—

If the voluntary principle were adopted in regard to Ireland, I do not see how we could long refuse an enquiry into the number of Dissenters in the United Kingdom, and the utility of the Church Establishment altogether. *The system, therefore, which I should be disposed to adopt, would be one which would put the Established Church, as regards the Roman Catholics and Protestants and the Presbyterians of the North of Ireland, on a footing of perfect equality.**

I go on to state that I am aware of the difficulties attending the adoption of such a measure, and that, as an earnest of future intentions, I wished to see an improvement in the Ecclesiastical College of May-

* *Hansard*, vol. lxxii. Feb. 1844.

nooth. The Endowment of Maynooth was carried with my cordial support, in 1845.

In the course of the debate of 1844, Mr. Disraeli made a most remarkable speech. He vindicated the conduct of the Tory party towards Ireland; and beginning with Charles the First, showed how that sovereign had treated the Irish Roman Catholics.

He referred to a period two centuries before the year in which he was speaking, and immediately before the breaking out of the Civil War. He stated that at that time there was a majority of Roman Catholics in Parliament, and a majority of Roman Catholics in the Council of State; that the municipalities were full of Roman Catholics, and that many of the sheriffs were Roman Catholics. He quoted the journal of Sir William Brereton, who, having visited Ireland in 1636, had seen at Wexford the Protestant judge of assize carried to his church by the Papist mayor, who was then carried himself to his mass-house. Having referred to this state of things, he recorded the fact that, after the breaking out of the Civil War, Glamorgan, the king's agent, had entered into a treaty with the Convention of Kilkenny, then in arms against the English Parliament. By the secret articles of that treaty, which was ratified by King Charles, it was stipulated, said Mr. Disraeli, that the Roman Catholics should enjoy the same civil and political equality which they had done previously to the breaking out of the Civil War; and with reference to the Protestant and Catholic Church, there should be a recognised equality between the

two churches. He then laid down as a principle for
the present time, that we ought not to imitate in
Ireland the institutions of England; but instead of
mimetic corporations and jobbing grand juries, with
imitative benches of English magistrates, we ought to
have in Ireland a strong executive and an impartial
administration. After speaking of the dense and
distressed population, he thus concluded :—

That dense population in extreme distress inhabited an
island where there was an Established Church which was
not their Church, and a territorial aristocracy, the richest of
whom lived in distant capitals. Thus they had a starving
population, an absentee aristocracy, and an alien Church, and,
in addition, the weakest executive in the world. That was
the Irish question. Well, then, what would honourable
gentlemen say if they were reading of a country in that position? They would say, at once, the remedy is revolution. But
the Irish could not have a revolution; and why? Because
Ireland was connected with another and a more powerful
country. Then what was the consequence? The connection
with England thus became the cause of the present state of
Ireland. If the connection with England prevented a revolution, and a revolution were the only remedy, England logi-
cally was in the odious position of being the cause of all the
misery in Ireland. What, then, was the duty of an English
minister? To effect by his policy all those changes which a
revolution would do by force. That was the Irish question
in its integrity. . . . . The moment they had *a strong
executive, a just administration, and ecclesiastical equality,*
they would have order in Ireland, and the improvement of
the physical condition of the people would follow.*

Of these three requisites, the two first—a strong

* *Hansard*, vol. lxxii. p. 1016.

executive and a just administration—are at present possessed by Ireland. Why not give ecclesiastical equality? But these were not the only opinions given by Mr. Disraeli in that memorable speech. He said in the same speech, ' He did not at all understand the new morality of the House of Commons when gentlemen said, " It is extremely desirable to do so and so, but it is so very difficult; and then there are prejudices. What are we to do against prejudices?" Why everything great was difficult.'

Again, referring to the prevalent disposition to wait for what is called the expression of public opinion, before proposing any measure, he said:—

Opinions were afloat, the public mind was agitated, and no one who was in authority came forward to lead the people. As the natural consequence of such neglect, they combined together and carried their own crude notions into effect; because nothing was clearer than this, that *if the Government did not lead the people, the people would drive the Government.* The time has gone by when a minister could with safety substitute the fulfilment of the duties of office for the performance of the functions of Government.*

These are, in my opinion, sound maxims, eloquently expressed. Yet I should be the last person to reproach Mr. Disraeli, if he hesitates to perform those functions of government which he declared cannot be safely neglected, and declines to establish that ecclesiastical equality which he proclaimed to be the talisman by which order would be produced, and the physical condition of the people improved.

* *Hansard,* vol. xvi. p. 1844.

I should be the last person, I say, who would reproach Mr. Disraeli, if he hesitates or shrinks from this great task. For I have myself, since 1844, held for more than twelve years important offices in the Government, and I have not attempted, during that time, to carry into effect opinions which in 1844, and on the grant to Maynooth in 1845, I had openly and distinctly avowed.

I have felt for the last quarter of a century that if I were to try to introduce religious equality in Ireland, I should be opposed by the Tory party as a solid phalanx, and that they would be assisted by a considerable defection from my own party. I should thus have injured, and not promoted, the cause of religious equality. The position of Mr. Disraeli is different from mine. He has boasted in the presence of the Lord Mayor and the merchants of the City of London, that he would not permit the Liberal party to have the monopoly of liberal measures. At Edinburgh he has declared that he has for seven years educated the Tory party, and has taught them successfully the grammar of household suffrage. Surely, therefore, we may expect that so easy a lesson as that of Ecclesiastical Equality in Ireland, the *pons asinorum* of political geometry, must have been mastered by all the more intelligent of his pupils.

But the question arises, ought the Irish people and their representatives to allow the Ministry, as Lord Stanley suggests, another year for further instruction from the great professor? No; let us say decidedly, No. For the question is one which will not brook delay, and the interests of Ireland must not be postponed to suit the convenience of any political party.

We cannot, therefore, accept the Bristol stone offered us by Lord Stanley as a real diamond.

If we are determined with Lord Stanley, and in conformity with the declarations of Lord Althorp, to resist the Repeal of the Union as the dismemberment of the Empire, we must make that Union the union of the two nations, as well as of the two legislatures. If we do not postpone executions, we must not postpone redress of grievances. If we are prompt to enforce implicit obedience, we must be prompt to lay the foundations of permanent peace.

We cannot indeed accede to the proposal for the Repeal of the Union, started by the Catholic clergy at Limerick, and supported by a great number of their body. There can be little hope in these days that an Irish House of Commons, meeting in Dublin, would act in harmony with a British House of Commons meeting at Westminster. They would, in all probability, act on views of vengeance, and a very narrow-minded nationality. They would very soon confiscate all property held by Englishmen, and even by Irishmen who would not renounce their residences in England. England would resent these acts. In short, a single session of the Irish Parliament would probably produce eternal separation between the two countries.

Yet even from the Limerick Declaration some hope may be derived.

In that Declaration it is said,—

A land tenure will accomplish something; the removal of the Protestant ascendency, by placing the Protestant Church in the same position before the State as the Catholic Church, will do much.

A measure *that will do much*, and which is strictly consonant with the. demands of justice, surely requires immediate attention.

It would therefore be folly to increase the discontent of Ireland by delay, and vague promises of some All hail! hereafter!

There is likewise something in the position of Lord Derby and Mr. Disraeli which repels absolute confidence. If the question is postponed till next year, the Tory party, whether forming a majority or a strong minority in the new House of Commons, may come from their elections, so invigorated by hustings' speeches, and so intoxicated by the old Tory policy of Lord Eldon, as to refuse to their leaders any reduction of the Irish Church Establishment.

It may be said, indeed, and has been said at the Bristol banquet, that in asking for the redress of Irish grievances, we are seeking a party purpose.

The following extract from a speech of the Right Hon. Gathorne Hardy will show with how much precision the polished weapons of party warfare may be wielded:—

There is a great letter-writer in England; he might almost be called a complete letter-writer. I allude to Earl Russell, who at all times, when he is out of office, seems to wonder how it is possible that the government of the country

can go on without him. (Laughter.) We had a ' Corn Law
Letter.' Then we had the Durham Letter. Now I see
advertised ' A Letter from Earl Russell to the Right Hon.
C. Fortescue on the State of Ireland.' We all know what
that means. (Hear, hear.) That trumpet may be blown;
it was blown once last Session, on the subject of education,
but so feebly that it came to nothing. But now it means
that we are to have the old faction cries, and that Ireland is
to be made a battle-ground, not for its own sake, but for the
sake of party strife.

We must be indifferent to these sarcasms. We are
fated to show the way of Reform to Tory Ministers.
So it has been with Catholic Emancipation; with the
Corn Laws; with the Reform Act of 1867. For
fifteen years we preached in vain that the admission
of the working classes to the franchise was required
by the state of society, and that it would strengthen
the Constitution.

Let me take an illustration.

When our troops landed in Abyssinia, it was found
that the mountain paths were so obstructed by rocks,
and were so narrow, that the horses, mules, and
animals of inferior dignity could not pass along them.
Engineers and pioneers were sent forward, and
smooth wide roads were made, along which all the
animals can pass. We Liberals are these engineers
and pioneers. And as the horses and mules and animals of inferior dignity, when they reached the green
pastures and clear streams, were heard to neigh and
bray with delight, so the party for whom we have
smoothed the rocks, and opened the road to the pas-

tures and the streams, were heard to huzza, to cheer, and to yell at the Bristol banquet.

There is one difference. Sir Robert Napier has, in handsome terms, thanked the engineers for opening the roads for his beasts of burthen; whereas those for whom we cleared away the obstacles find a pleasure in heaping abuse and foul language upon Mr. Gladstone and Mr. Bright, and the rest of the Liberals who have been the pioneers of Reform. So that when Mr. Hardy goes to seek for re-election at Oxford, he may boast of having swept away the Irish clergy, and gain great applause by the abuse he will not fail to cast upon you and me as aiming at no less than the ruin of the Church, and a change in the Home Office!

Let us turn, before I conclude, to the state of the Empire, and observe how many favourable auspices combine for the settlement of this question. England's strength is England's opportunity.

If, then, we look to trade and finance, and perceive a Chancellor of the Exchequer exulting in the resources which Mr. Gladstone had derived from the creative power of his genius, and bequeathed to his successor, we may say, *Miraturque novas frondes et non sua poma.*

In regard to foreign affairs, while peace has been unbroken, Lord Stanley has not shrunk from maintaining, in the Luxemburg Convention, that old foreign policy which led to greatness and to fame, from the days of Lord Burleigh to those of Lord Palmerston; nor while he has shown every disposition to conciliate the United States, has he been slow to assert the right of this nation to be treated as an independent power. Our armaments, carefully prepared by the late Government, and continued by the present, are ready to meet any enemy, and capable of being rapidly increased, should the necessity arise.

From various parts of the Queen's dominions, from the Queen's son in Australia, from the Queen's representative in Canada, come the expressions of loyalty to the Government, and affection to the person of our Sovereign.

One dark spot alone casts a shadow over the brightness of this prospect. One failure alone points the sarcasm of critics envious of our glory, or hostile to our freedom. That spot is the Church in Ireland. Let us redress that grievance. Never were nations more fitted to cling together than England, Scotland, and Ireland. Let Ireland obtain what Scotland demanded and obtained. Let us not sever the union of these nations, famous alike for valour and for ability.

The English have the most perseverance, the Scotch the most sense, the Irish the most generosity. But all these nations, speaking one language, living in two islands closely connected; governed by a mixed race of Norman, Saxon, and Celt, are destined to form, as they have formed, through dangers, convulsions, and disasters, a community, or, if you will, an empire, distinguished by its high spirit, its freedom, and its civilisation. Let us only add Hibernia Pacata to our victories of peace, and the future may exceed the past.